MW01487944

# Go Make (Pentecostal) Disciples

Ray James

GO MAKE (PENTECOSTAL) DISCIPLES
Dr. Raymond O. James, III

Published By Parables
July 2018



Unless otherwise specified Scripture quotations are taken from the authorized version of the King James Bible.

ISBN 978-1-945698-67-5
Printed in the United States of America

Readers should be aware that Internet Web sites offered as citations and/or sources for further information may have been changed or disappeared between the time this was written and when it is read.

# Go Make (Pentecostal) disciples

Ray James

***What others are saying about Go Make (Pentecostal) Disciples:***

"Dr. Ray James has written a must-read for discipleship... read this book - and learn from a Pentecostal perspective the easy-to-use strategy, laid out in a 52 chapter/week format. This book is a gift to the church and pastors who are mentoring others on their spiritual journey."

**Dr. Tim R. Barker**
**District Superintendent South Texas District Assemblies of God, Houston, TX**

"Over the next 52 weeks, this book gives you the opportunity to take quantum leaps forward in your spiritual development. Intentional Pentecostal discipleship is a process of developing passionate followers of Jesus Christ who are continually being empowered by the Holy Spirit. Unfortunately, casual Sunday morning attenders who are Biblically illiterate, spiritually inept, and culturally conformed are predominately populating too many churches. If you want to avoid spiritual malnutrition, which occurs as a result of drinking the milk instead of consuming the meat of the Word, then this 52-week study has been designed just for you. Become a strong Pentecostal disciple yourself and multiply by developing strong Pentecostal disciples!"

**Rev. Terry G. Bailey**
**District Superintendent, Tennessee Assemblies of God Ministry Network**

With passion, conviction and skill Dr. James has provided a teachable model for Pentecostal discipleship in a one-year weekly format. I recommend it as a resource for pastors to place in the hands of those who are called to teach in the local church.

**Dr. H. Robert Rhoden**
**Author of FOUR FACES OF A LEADER**

"In his excellent book, 'Go Make (Pentecostal) Disciples' Dr. Ray James presents a very clear definition of the biblical term and then provides an amazing resource for Pastors, church leaders, and all Christians, who truly desire to fulfill the Great Commission. This book can be used individually or as part of a small group resource or discipleship class. It includes 52 clear lessons that cover essential components of the discipleship journey and it effectively addresses necessary doctrinal issues including our Pentecostal distinctives. It is comprehensive, yet it is also simple and easy to read and teach. My sincere hope is that many will make use of this important resource! I pray that we will once again commit ourselves to fulfillment of the Great Commission to 'Make Disciples'."

**Rev. Wes Bartel**
**Former Director of Discipleship Ministries for Assemblies of God**

"Go Make (Pentecostal) Disciples" is a great teaching resource that categorizes much of the scriptures as biblical foundations for basic evangelical Christian doctrines, which are taught by Pentecostal churches and denominations. It is structured in such a way that it can be easily used for instruction as a discipleship doctrinal training course over a period of 12 months (52 weeks). At the conclusion of each lesson, practical application of the truths addressed may be incorporated in the process of personal discipleship as well as by encouraging engagement in an ongoing process of making disciples of Christ. I would certainly recommend this book as a helpful resource to facilitate the disciple making efforts of any local church.

**Rev. Ted Coody**
**Lead Pastor, Greenville First Pentecostal Holiness Church**

# ABOUT THE AUTHOR

Reverend James is an ordained minister, and has pastored in Illinois, Pennsylvania, Maryland, and Virginia. He has a Bachelor's Degree in Theology, a Master's in Pastoral Ministry, and a Doctorate in Ministry. He and his wife, Linda, reside in North Carolina. They have two adult children, eight grandchildren, and four great-grandchildren.

# DEDICATION

Dedicated to my wife, Linda, of over 48 years.
You have patiently forgiven me for spending many
hours shut up in my home office… writing.
Your tolerance is appreciated more than you know.
I pray tens of thousands are discipled as a result
of your long-suffering during this process.

# TABLE OF CONTENTS

"GO MAKE (PENTECOSTAL) DISCIPLES"

# Chapter 1
## Preface

There was urgency in our Lord's voice that day as He appointed those gathered to this great task. His commission was not a suggestion, but rather interpreted as more of a military command: "Go Make Disciples".

From that hillside gathering, He went to meet with His disciples and instructed them to wait for the empowering of the Holy Spirit, Who would enable them to complete their assigned task.

Within minutes, earth's gravity released the body of Jesus to ascend into heaven and to be seated at the right hand of God, our Father.

Nearly 6,000 years have passed since that day, and many lives have been given to fulfill our Savior's command. A command passed down through the generations that have followed. Nevertheless, a command that seems to have lost its urgency in our world today.

During my decades of ministry, I have witnessed a decrease of evangelism, and the desire of nominal Christians to lead others to Christ, and teach them to be authentic disciples of Jesus Christ. We must make evangelism a priority in the church again. Everyone has friends, relatives, business associates, acquaintances, and neighbors they can invite to church. However, we must not forsake them at the altar when they accept Jesus as their Savior. We must begin to intentionally disciple them. We must have purposeful "next steps" to mature these people in their new faith.

While it is true that all denominations, fellowships, and churches have their own statements of faith, position papers and core doctrines, it has been my observation that these documents have been used more as a standard for belief and membership, than as an instrument for discipleship.

Accordingly, it is my prayer that this book will guide you

through a disciple-making process using the disciplines of Pentecostal distinctives, with additional topics included.

In our churches, small groups, Christian education classes, men's groups and women's groups, may we return to pouring our life into others, as Paul did with Timothy, and make disciples.

It is my prayer and objective, that the format of this book will make it easier to teach our Pentecostal distinctives, to those we are discipling.

# Chapter 2
# Introduction

Remember, Christian discipleship is about teaching a person how to be a follower of Jesus Christ. Although this book is written in a 52-chapter format, to help guide the reader through a one-year process of discipling, by no means would I suggest it covers everything that should be taught in the discipleship process. Likewise, depending on the immediate needs of the reader, whether a disciple or disciple-maker, it may be prudent to skip to a chapter that he or she has an urgent need for understanding.

For example, if a person has just accepted Jesus Christ as their Lord and Savior and has an illness or infirmity in their body, you may want to skip to the chapter on Divine Healing first. If a person has been a Christian for a longer period, but never discipled, and has a desire to be baptized in the Holy Spirit, you may want to jump to those chapters first, and then come back to the beginning.

Please notice also that there are times in some of the chapters where I am quoting from my church's Statement of Fundamental Truths, where I will add my own thoughts and comments to a Statement. To differentiate my comments from the original Statement (in those chapters) I will italicize my comments.

If your thoughts wander in a particular chapter, or on a particular topic, do not be concerned about that. The objective of this book is simply to give intentionality to discipling, with emphasis on Pentecostalism. This is only a starting point, it is certainly not to be considered all that can, or should, be covered.

Listen to the person you are discipling, and help them understand God's Word on any issue they are facing.

Take a few minutes this week to look at the Chapter titles, and discuss the importance of each of these topics to the discipleship process.

Pray together before each week's session, and ask the Holy Spirit to direct your thoughts.

# Chapter 3
## Defining

Revelation 4:11 tells us, "Thou art worthy, O Lord, to receive glory and honour and power: for thou hast created all things, and for thy pleasure they are and were created."

All of the cares of this world often overwhelm us, financially, emotionally, and physically, so much so that we forget our life; but living was never intended to be about us. In reality, our life is to be all about Him, our Creator, our Lord, and our Savior.

Scripture tells us, "...and for thy pleasure [we] are created." The obvious question then, that is begging to be answered, is: What would bring God pleasure? I believe the answer to that question begins with John 3:16, "For God so loved the world, that he gave his only begotten Son, that whosoever believeth in him should not perish, but have everlasting life."

God loves all people, and He has given His Son, Jesus, to die for us, so that we may have everlasting life. Not just for us, but also for "whosoever believeth in him".

Wouldn't you agree that the greatest pleasure we could give to God would be to tell others of His love for them? Witnessing and evangelism are actually the first step in discipleship. We are to share our faith and tell nonbelievers about the wonderful changes Jesus Christ has made in our life. No matter what our maturity level in the Christian life, we have something to offer. Too often, we believe the lie from Satan that we don't really know enough or haven't been a Christian long enough to make a difference. Not true! Some of the most enthusiastic representatives of the Christian life are new believers who have just discovered the awesome love of God. They may not know a lot of Bible verses or the "accepted" way of saying things, but they have experienced the love of the living God, and that is exactly what we are to share.

By definition, a disciple is a follower, a pupil, one who accepts and assists in spreading the doctrines of another. A Christian disciple is a person who accepts and assists in spreading the good news of Jesus Christ. Christian discipleship is the process by which disciples grow in the Lord Jesus Christ and are equipped by the Holy Spirit, who resides in our hearts, to overcome the pressures and trials of this present life and become more Christ-like.

As you read this book, which has been divided into a 52-week study, you will notice that it is written in bite-sized segments to help you to understand what God has done for you, and what He desires of you, to bring others along with you on this discipleship journey.

Dictionaries and reference books define discipleship as "a person who is a pupil or an adherent of the doctrines of another." Christian discipleship then, would be, a person who is a pupil or believer in the doctrines of Jesus Christ. To this point, everyone seems to have a list of various methods and strategies for making disciples.

Instead of trying to separate the confusion of what others say discipleship should be, why don't we simply use God's Word, the Bible, as the source for determining what the principles of discipleship should be?

First, let's recognize that a disciple is what Jesus demonstrated to those He discipled. You may recall His disciples called Him teacher. That is exactly what a disciple needs, a personal instructor, a mentor; who will make a personal commitment through a personal relationship with the one(s) they are discipling (instructing to be a follower of Jesus Christ.)

Consider with me the words of Jesus found in Matthew's gospel, chapter 28, and verses 18-20. His commandment was to "Go Make Disciples". We know this passage of scripture to be the Great Commission:

> " And Jesus came and spake unto them, saying, All power is given unto me in heaven and in earth. Go ye therefore, and teach all nations, baptizing them in the name of the Father, and of the Son, and of the Holy Ghost: Teaching them to observe all things whatsoever I have commanded you: and, lo, I am with you always, even unto the end of the world. Amen."

Jesus begins by saying, "All power is given unto me in heaven and in earth." What He was saying is, I am about to tell you something that is rooted and grounded in the fact of my absolute authority over everything… so, pay close attention. With that said, and settled, He told them to go make disciples. Baptize those who believe, and teach them to be obedient to everything I have taught you. And, He says, I'll be with you.

Simply put, the disciple-maker (teacher) is to instruct the disciple (pupil/follower) in the principles (not laws) of a God Who loves them, modeling the example that Jesus Christ has given us through His Holy Word.

# CHAPTER 4
## DIVINE PLAN

In both Matthew's gospel (4:19), and Mark's gospel (1:17), Jesus told His disciples to, "Come follow me, and I will make you fishers of men."

Certainly, those words would catch the interest of fishermen. Fishers of men?

In the Great Commission, we can see that discipleship is about every Christian becoming a disciple-maker… not just a disciple. Jesus discipled His followers by teaching them to become disciple-makers, fishers of men. That is evangelism, the first step of Discipleship.

In everything that Jesus taught His disciples, He was giving a divine example of how to perpetuate the disciple-making process; and there is only one way, His way.

There are many churches today that will claim their Sunday school, Christian education, small groups, and such, are the discipleship arm of their church. However, when pressed to explain the methodology and strategy for making disciples, the leadership normally flounders with words of how much God loves us, and how we are to share the love of God with others, as Jesus shared His love for the world.

While this is understandable, it is certainly not the complete plan Jesus intended when He gave the Great Commission to His disciples.

Admitedly, evangelism is the first step in the discipleship process, but it was never intended to be the end of the process. The goal of discipleship is to reach people for Christ, but that is only the beginning. The ultimate goal is to ensure those reached accept Jesus as their personal Lord and Savior, and, then, are instructed (discipled) to lead others to Christ, and make disciple-makers also of them, and continue to perpetuate that process.

This divine plan is the way Jesus intended the gospel to be spread to the four-corners of the globe.

Just as Jesus came into the world, and chose twelve men to follow Him, so He could pour His life into them, He also chose three of them for a closer, more intimate relationship. Today, pastors, and missionaries at home and abroad, will preach to the masses, but they will also build relationships with a few, and separate those few for interpersonal relationships of instruction.

The objective of this close, interpersonal relationship, is to grow each individual to a level of spiritual maturity to lead that person from being a disciple, to being a disciple-maker.

The divine plan that Jesus modeled was not simply to get people ready to go to heaven, but, rather, to disciple them to disciple others to be ready to go to heaven, and take others with them.

His plan for disciple making is designed to reach the entire world. Let me illustrate this another, simpler way. I reach you and disciple you to go out and evangelize. Then the two of us reach two more, and replicate the process again. Now the four of us reach four more, and the eight of us reach eight, and sixteen reach sixteen, thirty-two reach thirty-two, 64, 128, 256, 512, 1024, 2048, 4096, 8192, 16,384... you get the picture. At that rate, the entire planet would have been reached long ago... if the church had obeyed the Great Commission.

Many churches have faith-walks and bible-talks, but have never had a discipleship plan.

This week ask yourself a few questions:

1. What is the only way to fulfill the Great Commission?

2. Has God already laid someone on your heart to disciple?

3. Are you willing to be obedient to God's directive?

4. Will you spend this next year reading and praying through this book, and your Bible?

5. Will you bring someone with you on this journey?

# CHAPTER 5
# DISCIPLESHIP BEGINS WITH EVANGELISM

There are many people today attending churches, who believe it is solely the pastor's responsibility to bring people to the church. If he or she has a staff, then it is "their" responsibility to do everything that needs to be done.

Fortunately, there are some in our churches that realize the pastor needs help, and they volunteer to teach a class or cook a dinner (when it's convenient for them.)

Then, there are others, who realize God has called, and gifted them, to perform a ministry in the church. Did you catch that word? Ministry! It's not simply a volunteer position to be flippantly approached; it's a "ministry" that God has called you to.

However, many view their "ministry" as being confined within the walls of the church, and no further.

To the common people in the audience, Jesus said, as recorded in Matthew 28:19, "Go… make disciples of all nations." You say, "I can't do that. I'm not trained." Dr. Luke has an answer for that, found in Acts 1:8: "… you shall receive power when the Holy Spirit has come upon you; and you shall be my witnesses…". Again, to the common people, Jesus said, I will equip you to do what I have called you to do.

No matter who you are, if you have accepted Jesus Christ as your Lord and Savior, it is your responsibility to "go make disciples". No exceptions. No excuses. Your "Lord" has spoken, and He desires your obedience. You have fellow students, friends, relatives, business associates, neighbors, and others I'm sure, whom you know that have not submitted their lives to Jesus Christ. One day God will hold us accountable for their lost soul. The Bible says:

**Ezekiel 33:8-9 (KJV)**

8 When I say unto the wicked, O wicked man, thou shalt surely die; if thou dost not speak to warn the wicked from his way, that wicked man shall die in his iniquity; but his blood will I require at thine hand. 9 Nevertheless, if thou warn the wicked of his way to turn from it; if he does not turn from his way, he shall die in his iniquity; but thou hast delivered thy soul.

The responsibility to reach the lost (evangelism), and witness to them of God's love, and the sacrifice of His Son, Jesus Christ, to redeem them from sin, is every Christian's duty.

If God is not willing for anyone to die in his or her sins, why should we be? Why would we want to see our friends, relatives, business associates, acquaintances, or neighbors die and miss heaven?

Jesus said:

**Matthew 9:36-38 (KJV)**

36 But when he saw the multitudes, he was moved with compassion on them, because they fainted, and were scattered abroad, as sheep having no shepherd. 37 Then saith he unto his disciples, the harvest truly is plenteous, but the labourers are few; 38 Pray ye therefore the Lord of the harvest, that he will send forth labourers into his harvest.

Jesus is the Great Shepherd, and when He saw those who had not accepted Him as their Lord and Savior, He was moved with compassion on them. Are we moved with compassion on the lost? If we are Christian, and by definition Christ-like, we should be.

My friend, evangelism begins with us, going into the harvest field all around us, in our schools, our places of business, our neighborhood, and at our family reunions (just to name a few places), and telling others of the good news of how much Jesus loves them.

Men's groups, Women's groups, Small Groups, and Senior Adult Ministries are all excellent places to invite our unsaved acquaintances to. Places where they can be loved and accepted. Places where they can meet other Christians, and see the changes God has made in their lives. Then, as the Holy Spirit draws them to Him, they will yield their lives to the Lordship of Jesus Christ, and they can begin the discipleship process, and, one day become a disciple-maker themselves.

Take a few minutes this week and begin to make a list of your friends, relatives, business associates, neighbors, and others that you could invite to a special event at your church, where they won't feel "threatened" and uncomfortable by their unsaved lifestyle. Begin praying for them, and watch for the Holy Spirit to open a door for your invitation. Do it now.

# CHAPTER 6
# THE HARVEST IS READY

I love living in the southeast. Farming is probably the biggest industry in this region. Every spring I watch as the farmers prepare their fields for planting; and then, we wait, and watch for the hundreds of thousands of acres of crops to ripen, and be ready for harvesting. Not all crops are planted at the same time, and, not all crops are ready to be harvested at the same time. But there are signs that indicate it's time to harvest.

There are also signs in humanity that alert us to the time of harvesting.

Last week we looked at **Matthew 9:36-38 (KJV)**

36 But when he saw the multitudes, he was moved with compassion on them, because they fainted, and were scattered abroad, as sheep having no shepherd. 37 Then saith he unto his disciples, The harvest truly is plenteous, but the labourers are few; 38 Pray ye therefore the Lord of the harvest, that he will send forth labourers into his harvest.

The wars and rumors of wars, bombings and destruction all around us, serve to remind us of the nearness of the coming of the Lord. Today the harvest is still plenteous, and, regrettably, the laborers are still few.

Strife abounds. Drug and alcohol addiction is at an all-time high. Certainly, the harvest is ripe.

One does not have to look long and hard to see the harvest fields of souls that are ready to be brought into the kingdom of God. The key here is to recognize the time for harvest, and, equally important to take care during the harvest. When it is time to harvest crops the farmers are extremely careful not to harm their crops. There is a method and strategy they use to get the most out of their fields. If they harvest too soon, the crop will be useless and wasted… lost forever. If they wait until the time has passed to harvest, the crop will again be lost.

Although we should always live a Christian, and Christ-filled life, we should not attempt to "harvest" someone into the Kingdom if the time is not right. To do so often causes more harm than good.

Accordingly, I would suggest there is a method and strategy that Christians should use during the harvest of men, and it begins by staying prepared for the harvest. Stay prayed-up and in-tune with the prompting of the Holy Spirit.

We need to be sensitive to the leading of the Holy Spirit, to nudge us when the time is right. God will open a door at just the right time, and we need to be always ready to walk through that door. To do that we need to keep our "spiritual tanks" filled with the empowering of the Holy Spirit, and alert to what is happening.

If someone is having an emotional problem, we don't need to quote scriptures on how God will supply all of their financial needs. If there is a health issue, that is not the time to discuss how God wants to forgive them of their rebellious lifestyle.

Go through the door God is opening. In other words, use the circumstances that are presented at that particular time. Be sensitive to the current need(s). Be gentle, be genuine, be compassionate, be friendly. Follow the leading of the Holy Spirit.

Gently present a simple gospel message, with Bible verses to support your presentation. If you need to, carry a piece of paper in your wallet or purse with Bible verses to use in various situations. For example, health, finances, emotions, mental, and so forth.

At the end of your gospel presentation, offer an opportunity for this person to receive Christ as their Lord… their healer, their provider, their strength, as appropriate. Don't force a decision, but offer the opportunity. In addition, don't forget to follow-up, soon, and often.

Use simple words. Don't use Bible jargon. Don't try to impress this person with theological or doctrinal phrases. Use a vocabulary that he or she understands… and, again… be gentle.

If the person accepts Christ as their Savior, gently start to disciple that person as soon as it is practical.

This week, begin to pray for the Holy Spirit to increase your sensitivity to the harvest field of souls around you. Look for Bible helps that will assist you in making a list of scriptures for various situations that you might confront… financially, physically, emotionally, relationally, and so forth.

# CHAPTER 7
# THE SCRIPTURES INSPIRED

The Scriptures, both the Old and New Testaments, are verbally inspired of God and are the revelation of God to man, the infallible, authoritative rule of faith and conduct.

**2 Timothy 3:15-17 (KJV)**
15 And that from a child thou hast known the holy scriptures, which are able to make thee wise unto salvation through faith which is in Christ Jesus. 16 All scripture is given by inspiration of God, and is profitable for doctrine, for reproof, for correction, for instruction in righteousness: 17 That the man of God may be perfect, thoroughly furnished unto all good works.

*I find it very interesting to note that the word "inspiration" found in verse 16, in the Greek, is the same word found in the Hebrew of Genesis 2:7, "breathed".*

**1 Thessalonians 2:13 (KJV)**
13 For this cause also thank we God without ceasing, because, when ye received the word of God which ye heard of us, ye received it not as the word of men, but as it is in truth, the word of God, which effectually worketh also in you that believe.

*It is imperative that those whom we are discipling understand that as they read and study the Word of God, they are not merely reading words that man has written, but, rather, words that God has "breathed" through those who wrote the words, by the inspiration of the Holy Spirit.*

**2 Peter 1:21 (KJV)**

21 For the prophecy came not in old time by the will of man: but holy men of God spake as they were moved by the Holy Ghost.

*When we are reading the Word of God, we are not reading the thoughts of man, but rather the words that God Himself inspired man to write. The Creator of heaven and earth desires to speak to us through His Word. That is why He gave us His word, so we might be encouraged and spiritually grow through hearing and understanding the words contained in the greatest love letter ever written to man.*

*There was a time in my life, when I was stationed overseas in the United States Air Force, separated by a great distance from my wife. She would send me letters, love letters, and I would read and meditate on each of the words contained in those letters. I would read them, and reread them several times. Those letters expressed her love for me. The same as God's Word contains His love for us, as in John 3:16, "For God so loved the world...".*

*The Apostle Paul, writing to his young protégé, Timothy, said those words given to him (and to us) were profitable for doctrine, for reproof, for correction, and for instruction in righteousness (so that we might be in right standing with God).*

*Those whom we are discipling need to understand the Bible is not just another book, to be set on a shelf. It is the greatest instruction manual ever written, and given to us by God Himself. Contained within its pages are the remedies to all of life's "sicknesses", and the answers to all of life's questions.*

*The inspired, God-breathed, Word of God is foundational to the discipling process. Without it, we could not know the One Whom we are to follow. We may be able to know "of" Him; but I would submit to you that we could not KNOW Him without His Word.*

*Paul tells us to "study" to show ourselves approved unto God. (2 Timothy 2:15) That word in the Greek means to make an effort, to be earnest, to labor and give diligence.*

*We must ensure those we are discipling, and mentoring, understand the seriousness of making God's Word a priority in their life, and Christian walk.*

# CHAPTER 8
## THE ONE TRUE GOD
## (PART ONE)

*It would be nearly impossible to list the number of gods that are worshipped today in the world. If you were to Google a search for the names of other gods you would literally come up with thousands of names. With that understanding, may I encourage you to use other versions and translations of the Bible (in addition to what I have used) to more fully explore The One True God of Christianity; and how He is set apart from all the other gods of this world.*

*Please, do not try to rush through this chapter. Knowing The One True God is integral to a disciple's decision to follow Him.*

*One day, writing to the church in Philippi, the Apostle Paul cried out "That I might know Him..." Philippians 3:10. This chapter will help you to teach the person you are discipling how to know Him.*

The one true God has revealed Himself as the eternally self-existent "I AM," the Creator of heaven and earth and the Redeemer of mankind. He has further revealed Himself as embodying the principles of relationship and association as Father, Son and Holy Spirit.

**Deuteronomy 6:4 (KJV)**
4 Hear, O Israel: The Lord our God is one Lord:

**Isaiah 43:10-11 (KJV)**
10 Ye are my witnesses, saith the Lord, and my servant whom I have chosen: that ye may know and believe me, and understand that I am he: before me there was no God formed, neither shall there be after me. 11 I, even I, am the Lord; and beside me there is no

saviour.
He is God, and besides Him there is no other God.

**Matthew 28:19 (KJV)**
19 Go ye therefore, and teach all nations, baptizing them in the name of the Father, and of the Son, and of the Holy Ghost:

**Luke 3:22 (KJV)**
22 And the Holy Ghost descended in a bodily shape like a dove upon him, and a voice came from heaven, which said, Thou art my beloved Son; in thee I am well pleased.

## The Adorable Godhead

a. Terms Defined

The terms "Trinity" and "persons" as related to the Godhead, while not found in the Scriptures, are words in harmony with Scripture, whereby we may convey to others our immediate understanding of the doctrine of Christ respecting the Being of God, as distinguished from "gods many and lords many." We therefore may speak with propriety of the Lord our God who is One Lord, as a trinity or as one Being of three persons, and still be absolutely scriptural.

**Matthew 28:19 (KJV)**
19 Go ye therefore, and teach all nations, baptizing them in the name of the Father, and of the Son, and of the Holy Ghost:

**2 Corinthians 13:14 (KJV)**
14 The grace of the Lord Jesus Christ, and the love of God, and the communion of the Holy Ghost, be with you all. Amen.

**John 14:16-17 (KJV)**
16 And I will pray the Father, and he shall give you another
Comforter, that he may abide with you forever; 17 Even the Spirit
of truth; whom the world cannot receive, because it seeth him not, neither knoweth him: but ye know him; for he dwelleth with you, and shall be in you.

*May I also add one of my favorite scriptures, that incorporates not only "The Adorable Godhead", but also "The Scriptures Inspired" of Chapter 7:*

**1 John 5:7**
"For there are three that bear record in heaven, the Father, the Word, and the Holy Ghost: and these three are one."

And for an understanding of Who the Word is (letting Scripture interpret Scripture):

**John 1:1-3 (KJV)**
"In the beginning was the Word, and the Word was with God, and the Word was God."

The Word was the Son, Jesus.

b. Distinction and Relationship in the Godhead
Christ taught a distinction of Persons in the Godhead which He expressed in specific terms of relationship, as Father, Son, and Holy Spirit, but that this distinction and relationship, as to its mode is inscrutable and incomprehensible, because unexplained.

**Luke 1:35 (KJV)**
35 And the angel answered and said unto her, The Holy Ghost shall come upon thee, and the power of the Highest shall overshadow thee: therefore also that holy thing which shall be born of thee shall be called the Son of God.

**1 Corinthians 1:24 (KJV)**
24 But unto them which are called, both Jews and Greeks, Christ the power of God, and the wisdom of God.

**Matthew 11:25-27 (KJV)**
25 At that time Jesus answered and said, I thank thee, O Father, Lord of heaven and earth, because thou hast hid these things from the wise and prudent, and hast revealed them unto babes. 26 Even so, Father: for so it seemed good in thy sight. 27 All things are delivered unto me of my Father: and no man knoweth the Son, but the Father; neither knoweth any man the Father, save the Son, and he to whomsoever the Son will reveal him.

**Matthew 28:19 (KJV)**
19 Go ye therefore, and teach all nations, baptizing them in the name of the Father, and of the Son, and of the Holy Ghost:

**2 Corinthians 13:14 (KJV)**
14 The grace of the Lord Jesus Christ, and the love of God, and

the communion of the Holy Ghost, be with you all. Amen.

**1 John 1:3-4 (KJV)**

3 That which we have seen and heard declare we unto you, that ye also may have fellowship with us: and truly our fellowship is with the Father, and with his Son Jesus Christ.

4 And these things write we unto you, that your joy may be full.

# CHAPTER 9
# THE ONE TRUE GOD (PART TWO)

**The Adorable Godhead (continued)**

c. Unity of the One Being of Father, Son and Holy Spirit

Accordingly, therefore, there is that in the Father which constitutes him the Father and not the Son; there is that in the Son which constitutes Him the Son and not the Father; and there is that in the Holy Spirit which constitutes Him the Holy Spirit and not either the Father or the Son. Wherefore the Father is the Begetter, the Son is the Begotten, and the Holy Spirit is the one proceeding from the Father and the Son. Therefore, because these three persons in the Godhead are in a state of unity, there is but one Lord God Almighty and His name one.

**John 1:18 (KJV)**

18 No man hath seen God at any time, the only begotten Son, which is in the bosom of the Father, he hath declared him.

**John 15:26 (KJV)**

26 But when the Comforter is come, whom I will send unto you from the Father, even the Spirit of truth, which proceedeth from the Father, he shall testify of me:

**John 17:11 (KJV)**

11 And now I am no more in the world, but these are in the world, and I come to thee. Holy Father, keep through thine own

name those whom thou hast given me, that they may be one, as we are.

**John 17:21 (KJV)**

21 That they all may be one; as thou, Father, art in me, and I in thee, that they also may be one in us: that the world may believe that thou hast sent me.

**Zechariah 14:9 (KJV)**

9 And the Lord shall be king over all the earth: in that day shall there be one Lord, and his name one.

*Whereas man is a tripartite, having a body, soul and spirit, which can, and one day will be separated; God is a Triune, of Father, Son, and Holy Spirit, which are One and inseparable.*

d. Identity and Cooperation in the Godhead

The Father, the Son and the Holy Spirit are never identical as to Person; nor confused as to relation; nor divided in respect to the Godhead; nor opposed as to cooperation. The Son is in the Father and the Father is in the Son as to relationship. The Son is with the Father and the Father is with the Son, as to fellowship. The Father is not from the Son, but the Son is from the Father, as to authority. The Holy Spirit is from the Father and the Son proceeding, as to nature, relationship, cooperation and authority. Hence, neither Person in the Godhead either exists or works separately or independently of the others.

**John 5:17-30 (KJV)**

17 But Jesus answered them, My Father worketh hitherto, and
I work. 18 Therefore the Jews sought the more to kill him, because
he not only had broken the sabbath, but said also that God was his
Father, making himself equal with God. 19 Then answered Jesus
and said unto them, Verily, verily, I say unto you, The Son can do
nothing of himself, but what he seeth the Father do: for what things
soever he doeth, these also doeth the Son likewise. 20 For the Father
loveth the Son, and sheweth him all things that himself doeth: and
he will shew him greater works than these, that ye may marvel. 21
For as the Father raiseth up the dead, and quickeneth them; even
so the Son quickeneth whom he will. 22 For the Father judgeth no
man, but hath committed all judgment unto the Son: 23 That all
men should honour the Son, even as they honour the Father. He
that honoureth not the Son honoureth not the Father which hath sent
him. 24 Verily, verily, I say unto you, He that heareth my word,
and believeth on him that sent me, hath everlasting life, and shall

not come into condemnation; but is passed from death unto life. 25 Verily, verily, I say unto you, The hour is coming, and now is, when the dead shall hear the voice of the Son of God: and they that hear shall live. 26 For as the Father hath life in himself; so hath he given to the Son to have life in himself; 27 And hath given him authority to execute judgment also, because he is the Son of man. 28 Marvel not at this: for the hour is coming, in the which all that are in the graves shall hear his voice, 29 And shall come forth; they that have done good, unto the resurrection of life; and they that have done evil, unto the resurrection of damnation. 30 I can of mine own self do nothing: as I hear, I judge: and my judgment is just; because I seek not mine own will, but the will of the Father which hath sent me.

**John 5:32 (KJV)**

32 There is another that beareth witness of me; and I know that the witness which he witnesseth of me is true.

**John 5:37 (KJV)**

37 And the Father himself, which hath sent me, hath borne witness of me. Ye have neither heard his voice at any time, nor seen his shape.

**John 8:17-18 (KJV)**

17 It is also written in your law, that the testimony of two men is true. 18 I am one that bear witness of myself, and the Father that sent me beareth witness of me.

This week, pause often to consider the three distinct persons of the Godhead, being one, and inseparable.

When Jesus was walking on this earth, it was God walking on this earth.

When the Holy Spirit is talking to you, it is God talking to you.

Pretty awesome, isn't it?

# CHAPTER 10
# THE ONE TRUE GOD (PART THREE)

**The Adorable Godhead**

**(continued)**

e. The Title, Lord Jesus Christ

The appellation, "Lord Jesus Christ," is a proper name. It is never applied in the New Testament, either to the Father or to the Holy Spirit. It therefore belongs exclusively to the Son of God.

**Romans 1:1-3 (KJV)**

1 Paul, a servant of Jesus Christ, called to be an apostle,
separated unto the gospel of God, 2 (Which he had promised afore
by his prophets in the holy scriptures,) 3 Concerning his Son Jesus
Christ our Lord, which was made of the seed of David according to
the flesh;

**2 John 3 (KJV)**

3 Grace be with you, mercy, and peace, from God the Father, and from the Lord Jesus Christ, the Son of the Father, in truth and love.

f. The Lord Jesus Christ, God with Us

The Lord Jesus Christ, as to His divine and eternal nature, is the proper and only Begotten of the Father, but as to His human nature, He is the proper Son of Man. He is therefore, acknowledged to be both God and man; who because He is God and man is "Immanuel," God with us.

**Matthew 1:23 (KJV)**

23 Behold, a virgin shall be with child, and shall bring forth a son, and they shall call his name Emmanuel, which being interpreted is, God with us.

**1 John 4:2 (KJV)**

2 Hereby know ye the Spirit of God: Every spirit that confesseth that Jesus Christ is come in the flesh is of God:

**1 John 4:10 (KJV)**

10 Herein is love, not that we loved God, but that he loved us, and sent his Son to be the propitiation for our sins.

**1 John 4:14 (KJV)**

14 And we have seen and do testify that the Father sent the Son to be the Saviour of the world.

**Revelation 1:13 (KJV)**

13 And in the midst of the seven candlesticks one like unto the Son of man, clothed with a garment down to the foot, and girt about the paps with a golden girdle.

**Revelation 1:17 (KJV)**

17 And when I saw him, I fell at his feet as dead. And he laid his right hand upon me, saying unto me, Fear not; I am the first and the last:

g. The Title, Son of God

Since the name "Immanuel" embraces both God and man in the one Person, our Lord Jesus Christ, it follows that the title, Son of God, describes His proper deity, and the title, Son of Man, His proper humanity. Therefore, the title Son of God, belongs to the order of eternity, and the title, Son of Man, to the order of time.

**Matthew 1:21-23 (KJV)**

21 And she shall bring forth a son, and thou shalt call his name
Jesus: for he shall save his people from their sins. 22 Now all this
was done, that it might be fulfilled which was spoken of the Lord by
the prophet, saying, 23 Behold, a virgin shall be with child, and shall
bring forth a son, and they shall call his name Emmanuel, which
being interpreted is, God with us.

**2 John 3 (KJV)**

3 Grace be with you, mercy, and peace, from God the Father, and from the Lord Jesus Christ, the Son of the Father, in truth and love.

**1 John 3:8 (KJV)**

8 He that committeth sin is of the devil; for the devil sinneth from the beginning. For this purpose the Son of God was manifested, that he might destroy the works of the devil.

**Hebrews 7:3 (KJV)**

3 Without father, without mother, without descent, having neither beginning of days, nor end of life; but made like unto the Son of God; abideth a priest continually.

**Hebrews 1:1-13 (KJV)**

1 God, who at sundry times and in divers manners spake in time past unto the fathers by the prophets, 2 Hath in these last days spoken unto us by his Son, whom he hath appointed heir of all things, by whom also he made the worlds; 3 Who being the brightness of his glory, and the express image of his person, and upholding all things by the word of his power, when he had by himself purged our sins, sat down on the right hand of the Majesty on high: 4 Being made so much better than the angels, as he hath by inheritance obtained a more excellent name than they. 5 For unto which of the angels said he at any time, Thou art my Son, this day have I begotten thee? And again, I will be to him a Father, and he shall be to me a Son? 6 And again, when he bringeth in the firstbegotten into the world, he saith, And let all the angels of God worship him. 7 And of the angels he saith, Who maketh his angels spirits, and his ministers a flame of fire. 8 But unto the Son he saith, Thy throne, O God, is for ever and ever: a sceptre of righteousness is the sceptre of thy kingdom. 9 Thou hast loved righteousness, and hated iniquity; therefore God, even thy God, hath anointed thee with the oil of gladness above thy fellows. 10 And, Thou, Lord, in the beginning hast laid the foundation of the earth; and the heavens are the works of thine hands: 11 They shall perish; but thou remainest; and they all shall wax old as doth a garment; 12 And as a vesture shalt thou fold them up, and they shall be changed: but thou art the same, and thy years shall not fail. 13 But to which of the angels said he at any time, Sit on my right hand, until I make thine enemies thy footstool?

# CHAPTER 11
# THE ONE TRUE GOD
# (PART FOUR)

**The Adorable Godhead**
**(continued)**

h. Transgression of the Doctrine of Christ

Wherefore, it is a transgression of the Doctrine of Christ to say that Jesus Christ derived the title, Son of God, solely from the fact of the incarnation, or because of His relation to the economy of redemption. Therefore, to deny that the Father is a real and eternal Father, and that the Son is a real and eternal Son, is a denial of the distinction and relationship in the Being of God; a denial of the Father, and the Son; and a displacement of the truth that Jesus Christ is come in the flesh.

**2 John 9 (KJV)**

9 Whosoever transgresseth, and abideth not in the doctrine of Christ, hath not God. He that abideth in the doctrine of Christ, he hath both the Father and the Son.

**John 1:1 (KJV)**

1 In the beginning was the Word, and the Word was with God, and the Word was God.

**John 1:2 (KJV)**

2 The same was in the beginning with God.

**John 1:14 (KJV)**
14 And the Word was made flesh, and dwelt among us, (and we beheld his glory, the glory as of the only begotten of the Father,) full of grace and truth.

**John 1:18 (KJV)**
18 No man hath seen God at any time, the only begotten Son, which is in the bosom of the Father, he hath declared him.

**John 1:29 (KJV)**
29 The next day John seeth Jesus coming unto him, and saith, Behold the Lamb of God, which taketh away the sin of the world.

**John 1:49 (KJV)**
49 Nathanael answered and saith unto him, Rabbi, thou art the Son of God; thou art the King of Israel.

**1 John 2:22-23 (KJV)**
22 Who is a liar but he that denieth that Jesus is the Christ?
He is antichrist, that denieth the Father and the Son. 23 Whosoever
denieth the Son, the same hath not the Father: he that acknowledgeth the Son hath the Father also.

**1 John 4:1-5 (KJV)**
1 Beloved, believe not every spirit, but try the spirits whether
they are of God: because many false prophets are gone out into
the world. 2 Hereby know ye the Spirit of God: Every spirit that
confesseth that Jesus Christ is come in the flesh is of God: 3 And
every spirit that confesseth not that Jesus Christ is come in the flesh
is not of God: and this is that spirit of antichrist, whereof ye have
heard that it should come; and even now already is it in the world.
4 Ye are of God, little children, and have overcome them: because
greater is he that is in you, than he that is in the world. 5 They are of
the world: therefore speak they of the world, and the world heareth
them.

**Hebrews 12:2 (KJV)**
2 Looking unto Jesus the author and finisher of our faith; who for the joy that was set before him endured the cross, despising the shame, and is set down at the right hand of the throne of God.

i. Exaltation of Jesus Christ as Lord

The Son of God, our Lord Jesus Christ, having by Himself purged our sins, sat down on the right hand of the Majesty on high;

angels and principalities and powers having been made subject unto Him. And having been made both Lord and Christ, He sent the Holy Spirit that we, in the name of Jesus, might bow our knees and confess that Jesus Christ is Lord to the glory of God the Father until the end, when the Son shall become subject to the Father that God may be all in all.

**Hebrews 1:3 (KJV)**

3 Who being the brightness of his glory, and the express image of his person, and upholding all things by the word of his power, when he had by himself purged our sins, sat down on the right hand of the Majesty on high:

**1 Peter 3:22 (KJV)**

22 Who is gone into heaven, and is on the right hand of God; angels and authorities and powers being made subject unto him.

**Acts 2:32-36 (KJV)**

32 This Jesus hath God raised up, whereof we all are witnesses.
33 Therefore being by the right hand of God exalted, and having
received of the Father the promise of the Holy Ghost, he hath shed
forth this, which ye now see and hear. 34 For David is not ascended
into the heavens: but he saith himself, The Lord said unto my Lord,
Sit thou on my right hand, 35 Until I make thy foes thy footstool.
36 Therefore let all the house of Israel know assuredly, that God
hath made the same Jesus, whom ye have crucified, both Lord and
Christ.

**Romans 14:11 (KJV)**

11 For it is written, As I live, saith the Lord, every knee shall bow to me, and every tongue shall confess to God.

**1 Corinthians 15:24-28 (KJV)**

24 Then cometh the end, when he shall have delivered up the
kingdom to God, even the Father; when he shall have put down all
rule and all authority and power. 25 For he must reign, till he hath put
all enemies under his feet. 26 The last enemy that shall be destroyed
is death. 27 For he hath put all things under his feet. But when he
saith all things are put under him, it is manifest that he is excepted,
which did put all things under him. 28 And when all things shall be
subdued unto him, then shall the Son also himself be subject unto
him that put all things under him, that God may be all in all.

# CHAPTER 12
# THE ONE TRUE GOD (PART FIVE)

**The Adorable Godhead (continued)**

j. Equal Honor to the Father and to the Son

Wherefore, since the Father has delivered all judgment unto the Son, it is not only the express duty of all in heaven and on earth to bow the knee, but it is an unspeakable joy in the Holy Spirit to ascribe unto the Son all the attributes of Deity, and to give Him all honor and the glory contained in all the names and titles of the Godhead except those which express relationship (see Distinction and Relationship in the Godhead, Unity of the One Being of Father, Son and Holy Spirit , and Identity and Cooperation in the Godhead) and thus honor the Son even as we honor the Father.

**John 5:22-23 (KJV)**

22 For the Father judgeth no man, but hath committed all judgment unto the Son: 23 That all men should honour the Son, even as they honour the Father. He that honoureth not the Son honoureth not the Father which hath sent him.

**1 Peter 1:8 (KJV)**

8 Whom having not seen, ye love; in whom, though now ye see him not, yet believing, ye rejoice with joy unspeakable and full of glory:

**Revelation 5:6-14 (KJV)**

6 And I beheld, and, lo, in the midst of the throne and of the four beasts, and in the midst of the elders, stood a Lamb as it had been slain, having seven horns and seven eyes, which are the seven Spirits of God sent forth into all the earth. 7 And he came and took the book out of the right hand of him that sat upon the throne. 8 And when he had taken the book, the four beasts and four and twenty elders fell down before the Lamb, having every one of them harps, and golden vials full of odours, which are the prayers of saints. 9 And they sung a new song, saying, Thou art worthy to take the book, and to open the seals thereof: for thou wast slain, and hast redeemed us to God by thy blood out of every kindred, and tongue, and people, and nation; 10 And hast made us unto our God kings and priests: and we shall reign on the earth. 11 And I beheld, and I heard the voice of many angels round about the throne and the beasts and the elders: and the number of them was ten thousand times ten thousand, and thousands of thousands; 12 Saying with a loud voice, Worthy is the Lamb that was slain to receive power, and riches, and wisdom, and strength, and honour, and glory, and blessing. 13 And every creature which is in heaven, and on the earth, and under the earth, and such as are in the sea, and all that are in them, heard I saying, Blessing, and honour, and glory, and power, be unto him that sitteth upon the throne, and unto the Lamb for ever and ever. 14 And the four beasts said, Amen. And the four and twenty elders fell down and worshipped him that liveth for ever and ever.

**Philippians 2:8-9 (KJV)**

8 And being found in fashion as a man, he humbled himself, and became obedient unto death, even the death of the cross. 9 Wherefore God also hath highly exalted him, and given him a name which is above every name:

**Revelation 7:9-10 (KJV)**

9 After this I beheld, and, lo, a great multitude, which no man could number, of all nations, and kindreds, and people, and tongues, stood before the throne, and before the Lamb, clothed with white robes, and palms in their hands; 10 And cried with a loud voice, saying, Salvation to our God which sitteth upon the throne, and unto the Lamb.

**Revelation 4:8-11 (KJV)**

8 And the four beasts had each of them six wings about him; and they were full of eyes within: and they rest not day and night, saying, Holy, holy, holy, Lord God Almighty, which was, and is,

and is to come. 9 And when those beasts give glory and honour and thanks to him that sat on the throne, who liveth for ever and ever, 10 The four and twenty elders fall down before him that sat on the throne, and worship him that liveth for ever and ever, and cast their crowns before the throne, saying, 11 Thou art worthy, O Lord, to receive glory and honour and power: for thou hast created all things, and for thy pleasure they are and were created.

# CHAPTER 13
# THE DEITY OF THE LORD JESUS CHRIST

The Lord Jesus Christ is the eternal Son of God. The Scriptures declare:

His virgin birth,

**Matthew 1:23 (KJV)**
23 Behold, a virgin shall be with child, and shall bring forth a son, and they shall call his name Emmanuel, which being interpreted is, God with us.

**Luke 1:31 (KJV)**
31 And, behold, thou shalt conceive in thy womb, and bring forth a son, and shalt call his name Jesus.

**Luke 1:35 (KJV)**
35 And the angel answered and said unto her, The Holy Ghost shall come upon thee, and the power of the Highest shall overshadow thee: therefore also that holy thing which shall be born of thee shall be called the Son of God.

His sinless life,

**Hebrews 7:26 (KJV)**
26 For such an high priest became us, who is holy, harmless, undefiled, separate from sinners, and made higher than the heavens;

**1 Peter 2:22 (KJV)**
22 Who did no sin, neither was guile found in his mouth:

His miracles,

**Acts 2:22 (KJV)**
22 Ye men of Israel, hear these words; Jesus of Nazareth, a man approved of God among you by miracles and wonders and signs, which God did by him in the midst of you, as ye yourselves also know:

**Acts 10:38 (KJV)**
38 How God anointed Jesus of Nazareth with the Holy Ghost and with power: who went about doing good, and healing all that were oppressed of the devil; for God was with him.

His substitutionary work on the cross,

**1 Corinthians 15:3 (KJV)**
3 For I delivered unto you first of all that which I also received, how that Christ died for our sins according to the scriptures;

**2 Corinthians 5:21 (KJV)**
21 For he hath made him to be sin for us, who knew no sin; that we might be made the righteousness of God in him.

His bodily resurrection from the dead,

**Matthew 28:6 (KJV)**
6 He is not here: for he is risen, as he said. Come, see the place where the Lord lay.

**Luke 24:39 (KJV)**
39 Behold my hands and my feet, that it is I myself: handle me, and see; for a spirit hath not flesh and bones, as ye see me have.

**1 Corinthians 15:4 (KJV)**
4 And that he was buried, and that he rose again the third day according to the scriptures:

His exaltation to the right hand of God,

**Acts 1:9 (KJV)**
9 And when he had spoken these things, while they beheld, he

was taken up; and a cloud received him out of their sight.

**Acts 1:11 (KJV)**
11 Which also said, Ye men of Galilee, why stand ye gazing up into heaven? this same Jesus, which is taken up from you into heaven, shall so come in like manner as ye have seen him go into heaven.

**Acts 2:33 (KJV)**
33 Therefore being by the right hand of God exalted, and having received of the Father the promise of the Holy Ghost, he hath shed forth this, which ye now see and hear.

**Philippians 2:9-11 (KJV)**
9 Wherefore God also hath highly exalted him, and given him a name which is above every name: 10 That at the name of Jesus every knee should bow, of things in heaven, and things in earth, and things under the earth; 11 And that every tongue should confess that Jesus Christ is Lord, to the glory of God the Father.

**Hebrews 1:3 (KJV)**
3 Who being the brightness of his glory, and the express image of his person, and upholding all things by the word of his power, when he had by himself purged our sins, sat down on the right hand of the Majesty on high:

# CHAPTER 14
## THE FALL OF MAN

Man was created good and upright; for God said, "Let us make man in our own image, after our likeness." However, man by voluntary transgression fell and thereby incurred not only physical death but also spiritual death, which is separation from God.

*By one man, the first Adam, all men inherited his sin, and sinful nature. Moreover, according to Romans 3:23 "For all have sinned and come short of the glory of God."*

**Genesis 1:26-27 (KJV)**
26 And God said, Let us make man in our image, after our likeness: and let them have dominion over the fish of the sea, and over the fowl of the air, and over the cattle, and over all the earth, and over every creeping thing that creepeth upon the earth. 27 So God created man in his own image, in the image of God created he him; male and female created he them.

**Genesis 2:17 (KJV)**
17 But of the tree of the knowledge of good and evil, thou shalt not eat of it: for in the day that thou eatest thereof thou shalt surely die.

**Genesis 3:6 (KJV)**
6 And when the woman saw that the tree was good for food, and that it was pleasant to the eyes, and a tree to be desired to make one wise, she took of the fruit thereof, and did eat, and gave also unto her husband with her; and he did eat.

**Romans 5:12-19 (KJV)**
12 Wherefore, as by one man sin entered into the world,

and death by sin; and so death passed upon all men, for that all
have sinned: 13 (For until the law sin was in the world: but sin is
not imputed when there is no law. 14 Nevertheless death reigned
from Adam to Moses, even over them that had not sinned after the
similitude of Adam's transgression, who is the figure of him that
was to come. 15 But not as the offence, so also is the free gift. For
if through the offence of one many be dead, much more the grace
of God, and the gift by grace, which is by one man, Jesus Christ,
hath abounded unto many. 16 And not as it was by one that sinned,
so is the gift: for the judgment was by one to condemnation, but
the free gift is of many offences unto justification. 17 For if by one
man's offence death reigned by one; much more they which receive
abundance of grace and of the gift of righteousness shall reign in life
by one, Jesus Christ.) 18 Therefore as by the offence of one judgment
came upon all men to condemnation; even so by the righteousness
of one the free gift came upon all men unto justification of life. 19
For as by one man's disobedience many were made sinners, so by
the obedience of one shall many be made righteous.

# CHAPTER 15
## THE SALVATION OF MAN

Man's only hope of redemption is through the shed blood of Jesus Christ the Son of God.

The Conditions to Salvation:

Salvation is received through repentance toward God and faith toward the Lord Jesus Christ. By the washing of regeneration and renewing of the Holy Spirit, being justified by grace through faith, man becomes an heir of God, according to the hope of eternal life.

*I think it is important to note here that repentance is not simply being sorry for what you have done. True repentance is deciding to abandon your old way of living, and making a conscious decision to follow faithfully after Jesus. Leaving your sinful, self-absorbed, lifestyle and seeking a life of holiness and righteousness before God. Through the help of the Holy Spirit, that is what Jesus offers us, by His shed blood for us on Calvary. Here's more:*

**Luke 24:47 (KJV)**

47 And that repentance and remission of sins should be preached in his name among all nations, beginning at Jerusalem.

**John 3:3 (KJV)**

3 Jesus answered and said unto him, Verily, verily, I say unto thee, Except a man be born again, he cannot see the kingdom of God.

**Romans 10:13-15 (KJV)**

13 For whosoever shall call upon the name of the Lord shall
be saved.14 How then shall they call on him in whom they have not

believed? and how shall they believe in him of whom they have not heard? and how shall they hear without a preacher? 15 And how shall they preach, except they be sent? as it is written, How beautiful are the feet of them that preach the gospel of peace, and bring glad tidings of good things!

**Ephesians 2:8 (KJV)**
8 For by grace are ye saved through faith; and that not of yourselves: it is the gift of God:

**Titus 2:11 (KJV)**
11 For the grace of God that bringeth salvation hath appeared to all men,

**Titus 3:5-7 (KJV)**
5 Not by works of righteousness which we have done, but according to his mercy he saved us, by the washing of regeneration, and renewing of the Holy Ghost; 6 Which he shed on us abundantly through Jesus Christ our Saviour; 7 That being justified by his grace, we should be made heirs according to the hope of eternal life.

The Evidence of Salvation:
The inward evidence of salvation is the direct witness of the Spirit.

**Romans 8:16 (KJV)**
16 The Spirit itself beareth witness with our spirit, that we are the children of God:

The outward evidence to all men is a life of righteousness and true holiness.

**Ephesians 4:24 (KJV)**
24 And that ye put on the new man, which after God is created in righteousness and true holiness.

**Titus 2:12 (KJV)**
12 Teaching us that, denying ungodliness and worldly lusts, we should live soberly, righteously, and godly, in this present world;

*It was a sobering thought to me one day, when someone reminded me "a King died for me, to provide my salvation."*
*We should realize that "we" are the only Bible that some people may ever read. When they look at our life... our* <u>*new*</u> *life... that our*

*Savior and Redeemer has provided for us on Calvary's Cross, do they now see Jesus living in us?*

*Our salvation is the fullness, completeness, and wholeness of everything God has in store for us. Are we a living, breathing, reflection of God's salvation?*

*Does the world see God's love through us? Are we daily walking in righteousness and holiness before Him?*

*Our salvation came at a great cost to Him. Discipleship must teach that!*

# CHAPTER 16
## FORGIVENESS OF GOD

In this superficial world in which we live today, when someone wrongs us and later asks for forgiveness, we may say we forgive them, but we often keep the thought of the wrong-doing in the museum of our memory. That thought normally never leaves us. It's there, and many times it's there to stay forever.

Several times throughout the Bible we see the reality of God's forgiveness.

**Daniel 9:9**
"To the Lord our God belong mercies and forgivenesses, though we have rebelled against him;"

**Acts 26:18**
"To open their eyes, and to turn them from darkness to light, and from the power of Satan unto God, that they may receive forgiveness of sins, and inheritance among them which are sanctified by faith that is in me."

**Ephesians 1:7**
"In whom we have redemption through his blood, the forgiveness of sins, according to the riches of his grace;"

**Colossians 1:14**
"In whom we have redemption through his blood, even the forgiveness of sins:"

**Isaiah 43:25**
"I, even I, am he that blotteth out thy transgressions for mine own sake, and will not remember thy sins."

**Hebrews 8:12**

"For I will be merciful to their unrighteousness, and their sins and their iniquities will I remember no more."

**Hebrews 10:12-17**

"12 But this man, after he had offered one sacrifice for sins for ever, sat down on the right hand of God; 13 From henceforth expecting till his enemies be made his footstool. 14 For by one offering he hath perfected for ever them that are sanctified. 15 Whereof the Holy Ghost also is a witness to us: for after that he had said before, 16 This is the covenant that I will make with them after those days, saith the Lord, I will put my laws into their hearts, and in their minds will I write them; 17 And their sins and iniquities will I remember no more."

Throughout Scripture we are reminded that God does not, and I would submit to you "cannot", remember the sins He has forgiven of us.

Let me put it another way. God loves you. God loves me. God loves us. He loves us so much that He sent His Son to this earth to die for us. To pay the price for our redemption.

If God loves us enough to sacrifice His only Son to redeem us of our sin, wouldn't you imagine He would do anything else for us? Of course, He would do anything. Including forgiving us of our sins, and… as several Scriptures above tell us, He "will remember them no more".

So quit letting our enemy, Satan, try to convince you that God doesn't love you, and that He hasn't forgiven you of your sin, and hasn't forgotten your sins.

God loves you!!! He has forgiven you (if you have asked Him to, and have invited Him into your heart.) In addition, He has forgotten your sins! Period.

If you have ever struggled with whether God loves you, or whether He has forgiven you of your sins, then choose this week to walk in the knowledge and understanding that He has.

Go ahead… just make the choice to do that!

# CHAPTER 17
## POSITION IN JESUS CHRIST

It is my personal opinion that unless Christians understand their position in Jesus Christ, they will never be able to unlock the door to abundant Christian living. I am not speaking of prosperity here, I am speaking of walking in the fullness, completeness, and wholeness of what Jesus gave to them on the cross of Calvary.

Here is the way the Apostle Paul says it:

> "God, being rich in mercy, because of His great love with which He loved us, even when we were dead in our transgression, made us alive together with Christ (by grace you have been saved), and raised us up with Him, and seated us with Him in the heavenly places, in Christ Jesus, in order that in the ages to come He might show us the riches of His grace in kindness toward us in Christ Jesus." Ephesians 2:4-7

Allow me to paraphrase those verses: Everything Jesus is, you are. Everything Jesus has, you have. God has placed you and me in Christ Jesus. As the Father is in the Son, and the Son is in the Father, so are you and I in the Son. Grafted in by the shed blood of Jesus Christ, on the cross of Calvary. When God looks at you and me, as His blood-bought children, He sees the sinless perfection of His Son, Jesus.

We may still be struggling with the process of sanctification, but when God looks at us, He sees us as a perfectly finished product, blessed with every available spiritual blessing.

Look at what the Apostle Paul wrote to the church at Colossae:

> "Since you have been raised up with Christ, keep seeking the things above, where Christ is, seated at the right hand of God. Set your mind on the things above, not on the things that are on earth. For you have died and your life is hidden with Christ in God. When Christ, who is our life, is revealed, then you also will be revealed with Him in glory." Colossians 3:1-4

We have already been raised up with Christ, and hidden with Him, in God. Dead to self, and alive in Him.

I challenge you to walk in that truth this week.

# CHAPTER 18
## FOLLOWING JESUS

If our position is in Him, as we considered last week, then we must consciously and intentionally follow after Him every minute of every day.

Acts 17:28 says, "In Him we live and move, and have our being."

The New Living Translation says, "In Him we live and move and exist."

Our very existence is in following after Him. Look at how Jesus said it:

**Matthew 16:24-25 (KJV)**

24 Then said Jesus unto his disciples, If any man will come after me, let him deny himself, and take up his cross, and follow me.
25 For whosoever will save his life shall lose it: and whosoever will lose his life for my sake shall find it.

We must deny ourselves, take up our own cross (the symbol of crucifying our fleshly person), and follow Him. Because it is only by losing our own carnal life, that we can find our real life in Him.

We must seek Him first. (Matthew 6:33) "But seek ye first the kingdom of God, and his righteousness; and all these things shall be added unto you."

We must forget about our self, and trust Him for His plan, His purpose, and His provision for us.

As Jesus said in Matthew 6:25:

"Therefore I say unto you, Take no thought for your life, what ye shall eat, or what ye shall drink; nor yet for your body, what ye shall put on. Is not the life more than meat, and the body than raiment?"

God knows what we have need of, and He (Who has created all things, and is in total and perfect control of all things) knows exactly what we have need of, long before we ask Him.

How is all of this done? By faith!

Hebrews 11:1 tells us, "Now faith is the substance of things hoped for, and the evidence of things not seen." Let me interpret that another way, "Now faith is the reality of things hoped for, and the proof of things not seen."

The very first word in that verse is "Now". If your faith is not "now" faith, I would suggest it is not faith. Our faith in following after God should be for every minute of every day, and every day of our life. We simply seek Him by following after Him, and trust Him to meet all of our needs and heal all of our hurts.

Paul wrote to the church in Corinth, and told them, "…Eye hath not seen, nor ear heard, neither have entered into the heart of man, the things which God hath prepared for them that love him." 1 Co. 2:9 (And, may I hasten to add, "and for them who will follow hard after Him.")

Many people today are following after the things of this world, and most people are miserable.

At the time of our salvation, if "old things are passed away, and all things are becoming new", as 2 Corinthians 5:17 tells us, wouldn't it only make sense that we would also need to be following something "new", and forsake the old things we were following after? Sure.

That's what "discipleship" is all about. As a "pupil" of Jesus Christ, we are learning to follow after Him, lean upon Him, and put all of our trust and faith in Him. Why? Because "He cares for us." 1 Peter 5:7

As a believer of Jesus Christ… a follower of Jesus Christ… a disciple of Jesus Christ… we have begun an exciting journey of following Him.

This week ask yourself: Am I denying myself? Have I lost my life for His sake? Am I wholly trusting Him and following after Him? Am I willing to commit myself to the only One who knows what is best for me?

If you are, hang on for a life-changing relationship with the Creator of heaven and earth.

# CHAPTER 19
## THE LORDSHIP OF JESUS CHRIST

Revelation 19:16 says, "And on His robe and on His thigh He has a name written, KING OF KINGS AND LORD OF LORDS."

There is no room for debate or discussion about that. Jesus is Lord, whether you are aware of it or not; and He is the Lord of lords.

Do you realize that a "lord" has complete and absolute rule and authority over everything in his kingdom? Now, think about that. If you lived in a kingdom ruled by a "lord", and that lord asked you to do something, it would not be open for debate. You would either be expected to do what was asked, or… you would suffer the consequence of disobedience.

When you and I became a Christian, we immediately became submissive to the rule and authority of the Lord of the Kingdom of God, Jesus Christ. When we humble ourselves to His Lordship, we become the recipient of His blessings. If we do not humble our self to His Lordship and are disobedient to Him, we are condemned, and will be the recipient of His curse. (You may want to study the Biblical Law of Blessings and Curses.)

All people are under the Lordship of Jesus Christ. The unbeliever, unsaved, who rejects His Lordship is condemned. Those who have accepted His Lordship will receive His blessings.

Here's what the Disciple John had to say about this: "He that believeth on him is not condemned: but he that believeth not is condemned already, because he hath not believed in the name of the only begotten Son of God." John 3:18 KJV

Your appreciation for the sacrifice Jesus made for you, should make you want to be obedient to His Lordship, and please Him. Let me ask you: How would you feel if I "literally" just saved your life? Would you want to please me, in return, for what I had done for you? If the role were reversed, I would certainly want to thank and please you. May I remind you He, Jesus Christ, saved our life, and gave us so much more. He redeemed us from Satan's grip, and Satan is no longer our lord, but, rather, Jesus Christ, the Lord of lords, is our Lord and Savior.

As our Lord, will we fully trust Him by our obedience to Him? With all of the issues of life, we can go to our Lord and ask for direction, and He will guide us. But the truth is, sometimes we don't understand where He is leading us, and we are hesitant to follow His lordship.

Have you ever been there?

So we take what the Lord has said, and add that to the options and opinions we have already made, and then make a choice out of all of them. Let me say this clearly: His is NOT an opinion, nor should it be an option. His word to us is His will for us, and needs to be obeyed.

When we come before the Lord of our life, and ask for His help with any issues of life, we MUST be willing to be totally obedient to what He tells us… because He knows what is best for us. Period.

Let me go back to the beginning of this chapter: there is nothing to debate or discuss. He is the Lord, and the Lord has spoken, through His Word. Period.

He has spoken. Follow His leading, and live in His blessings.

This week ask yourself a couple of questions: Do you really want the Lord's will for your life, or, are you just searching for another option? If you really want His will for your life, are you willing to forsake your opinions and follow His will?

Listen for our Lord's direction. Sometimes He speaks through His Word, the Holy Bible. Sometimes He speaks through others: our pastors, friends, family, or others. Sometimes He simply nudges us through an intuitive way, as the Holy Spirit, dwelling within us, prompts us in a certain, unmistakable, direction.

# CHAPTER 20
# FELLOWSHIP WITH JESUS

As a minister, and as a pastor, I always enjoyed the times of fellowship I had with other ministers, and those of like precious faith. Likewise, I always enjoyed church dinners, where we could just get lost in conversations with others about what God had been doing in our lives that week. The time would go by so quickly.

What do you think? Would Jesus love to have fellowship with you? No questions about the issues of life. No direction regarding your family, your health, your job, your finances, or anything else. Just sitting and enjoying the presence of one another.

Now don't think I've completely lost it. Don't close the book, or skip to the next chapter.

Think about this. Do you enjoy going to family reunions, and just sitting around listening to different family members telling you stories about silly events in their lives?

May I remind you that when you became a Christian, you became a part of the family of God; and that family extends around the globe through the Body of Christ... His church. I would further suggest to you that each member in the Body of Christ is dependent upon each other.

The Apostle Paul tells the church at Ephesus, in Ephesians 4:16 (New Life Version) *16 Christ has put each part of the church in its right place. Each part helps other parts. This is what is needed to keep the whole body together. In this way, the whole body grows strong in love.*

Look at that again, "Each part helps other parts", and "Christ has put each part of the church in its right place", so that "the whole body grows strong in love".

Simply stated another way, I need you to do your part, and you need me to do my part, and others need us to do our parts, just as we need them to do their parts, so we can ALL grow strong in love, and God IS love. So, the intention is to grow in Him. If you, as a member of the church of Jesus Christ, are not doing your part, it will not only prevent me from growing, but it will stunt the growth of others in the body that are depending on you to use your spiritual gift(s) for their development. Do you see how important it is for you to know what your gift is, and to be engaged in using your gift?

Sometimes our spiritual gift(s) is delivered through our conversations with others. Maybe it is the gift of discernment, or faith, or helps, or mercy, or teaching, or wisdom. There are a number of ways we can use our spiritual gift(s), simply through conversation. Conversation to motivate and encourage, or support someone.

However, I believe one of the greatest blessings of fellowship is just in "hanging out" without having any sort of an agenda. Just chatting, and laughing… and sometimes crying.

It is probably a lost art in today's digital, tech driven, world that we live in. Most people today simply do not see the importance in forming personal relationships through fellowship. May I suggest the greatest personal relationship we could have is with our Lord and Savior, our heavenly Father, and His precious Holy Spirit. Just to sit in the presence of our spiritual family, and tell our hearts secrets to them… not that they don't already know all of our secrets.

I have two thoughts for this week:

1. Sit down and bask in the presence of your spiritual family, God the Father, God the Son, and God the Holy Spirit; and just enjoy their company for a while.

2. Take a Spiritual Gifts Survey, and update yourself on how God wants to use you, as you fellowship with Jesus, and, within the Body of Christ.

# CHAPTER 21
# THE ORDINANCES OF THE CHURCH

Baptism in Water

The ordinance of baptism by immersion is commanded by the Scriptures. All who repent and believe on Christ as Saviour and Lord are to be baptized. Thus they declare to the world that they have died with Christ and that they also have been raised with Him to walk in newness of life.

*Water baptism does not save us. It is simply the outward profession of an inward confession that we have accepted Jesus Christ as our Lord and Savior, in obedience to God's Word.*

**Matthew 28:19 (KJV)**

19 Go ye therefore, and teach all nations, baptizing them in the name of the Father, and of the Son, and of the Holy Ghost:

**Mark 16:16 (KJV)**

16 He that believeth and is baptized shall be saved; but he that believeth not shall be damned.

**Acts 10:47-48 (KJV)**

47 Can any man forbid water, that these should not be baptized, which have received the Holy Ghost as well as we? 48 And he commanded them to be baptized in the name of the Lord. Then prayed they him to tarry certain days.

**Romans 6:4 (KJV)**

4 Therefore we are buried with him by baptism into death: that

like as Christ was raised up from the dead by the glory of the Father, even so we also should walk in newness of life.

*Water baptism is by total immersion. As I previously mentioned, it is the outward profession of an inward confession of our salvation. When we are placed under the water, that is to symbolize our death (to self) with Jesus Christ. When we are raised out of the water, that is to typify our new life through Jesus. As the scripture says, "I am crucified with Christ: nevertheless I live; yet not I, but Christ liveth in me: and the life which I now live in the flesh I live by the faith of the Son of God, who loved me, and gave himself for me." Galatians 2:20*

The second ordinance of the church is:

Holy Communion

The Lord's Supper, consisting of the elements -- bread and the fruit of the vine -- is the symbol expressing our sharing the divine nature of our Lord Jesus Christ (2 Peter 1:4), a memorial of His suffering and death (1 Corinthians 11:26), and a prophecy of His second coming (1 Corinthians 11:26), and is enjoined on all believers "till He come!"

**2 Peter 1:4 (KJV)**
4 Whereby are given unto us exceeding great and precious promises: that by these ye might be partakers of the divine nature, having escaped the corruption that is in the world through lust.

**1 Corinthians 11:26 (KJV)**
26 For as often as ye eat this bread, and drink this cup, ye do shew the Lord's death till he come.

*No, the bread does not become the body of Christ, it merely symbolizes His body; and, the juice in the cup does not become the blood of Christ, it is simply symbolic of His blood.*

If you have not been baptized in water, I would encourage you to do so. Ask your pastor about that this week.

Also, the next time you partake of Communion, remember you are "showing the Lord's death, until He returns".

# CHAPTER 22
# THE BAPTISM IN THE HOLY SPIRIT (PART ONE)

All believers are entitled to and should ardently expect and earnestly seek the promise of the Father, the baptism in the Holy Spirit and fire, according to the command of our Lord Jesus Christ. This was the normal experience of all in the early Christian Church. With it comes the enduement of power for life and service, the bestowment of the gifts and their uses in the work of the ministry.

**Luke 24:49 (KJV)**
49 And, behold, I send the promise of my Father upon you: but tarry ye in the city of Jerusalem, until ye be endued with power from on high.

**Acts 1:4 (KJV)**
4 And, being assembled together with them, commanded them that they should not depart from Jerusalem, but wait for the promise of the Father, which, saith he, ye have heard of me.

**Acts 1:8 (KJV)**
8 But ye shall receive power, after that the Holy Ghost is come upon you: and ye shall be witnesses unto me both in Jerusalem, and in all Judaea, and in Samaria, and unto the uttermost part of the earth.

**1 Corinthians 12 (KJV)**
1 Now concerning spiritual gifts, brethren, I would not have

you ignorant. 2 Ye know that ye were Gentiles, carried away unto these dumb idols, even as ye were led. 3 Wherefore I give you to understand, that no man speaking by the Spirit of God calleth Jesus accursed: and that no man can say that Jesus is the Lord, but by the Holy Ghost. 4 Now there are diversities of gifts, but the same Spirit. 5 And there are differences of administrations, but the same Lord. 6 And there are diversities of operations, but it is the same God which worketh all in all. 7 But the manifestation of the Spirit is given to every man to profit withal. 8 For to one is given by the Spirit the word of wisdom; to another the word of knowledge by the same Spirit; 9 To another faith by the same Spirit; to another the gifts of healing by the same Spirit; 10 To another the working of miracles; to another prophecy; to another discerning of spirits; to another divers kinds of tongues; to another the interpretation of tongues: 11 But all these worketh that one and the selfsame Spirit, dividing to every man severally as he will. 12 For as the body is one, and hath many members, and all the members of that one body, being many, are one body: so also is Christ. 13 For by one Spirit are we all baptized into one body, whether we be Jews or Gentiles, whether we be bond or free; and have been all made to drink into one Spirit. 14 For the body is not one member, but many. 15 If the foot shall say, Because I am not the hand, I am not of the body; is it therefore not of the body? 16 And if the ear shall say, Because I am not the eye, I am not of the body; is it therefore not of the body? 17 If the whole body were an eye, where were the hearing? If the whole were hearing, where were the smelling? 18 But now hath God set the members every one of them in the body, as it hath pleased him. 19 And if they were all one member, where were the body? 20 But now are they many members, yet but one body. 21 And the eye cannot say unto the hand, I have no need of thee: nor again the head to the feet, I have no need of you. 22 Nay, much more those members of the body, which seem to be more feeble, are necessary: 23 And those members of the body, which we think to be less honourable, upon these we bestow more abundant honour; and our uncomely parts have more abundant comeliness. 24 For our comely parts have no need: but God hath tempered the body together, having given more abundant honour to that part which lacked. 25 That there should be no schism in the body; but that the members should have the same care one for another. 26 And whether one member suffer, all the members suffer with it; or one member be honoured, all the members rejoice with it. 27 Now ye are the body of Christ, and members in particular. 28 And God hath set some in the church, first apostles, secondarily prophets, thirdly teachers, after that miracles, then gifts of healings, helps, governments, diversities of tongues. 29 Are all apostles? are all prophets? are all teachers?

are all workers of miracles? 30 Have all the gifts of healing? do all
speak with tongues? do all interpret? 31 But covet earnestly the best
gifts: and yet shew I unto you a more excellent way.

# CHAPTER 23
# THE BAPTISM IN THE HOLY SPIRIT (PART TWO)

This experience (*the Baptism in the Holy Spirit*) is distinct from and subsequent to the experience of the new birth.

**Acts 8:12-17 (KJV)**

12 But when they believed Philip preaching the things concerning the kingdom of God, and the name of Jesus Christ, they were baptized, both men and women. 13 Then Simon himself believed also: and when he was baptized, he continued with Philip, and wondered, beholding the miracles and signs which were done. 14 Now when the apostles which were at Jerusalem heard that Samaria had received the word of God, they sent unto them Peter and John: 15 Who, when they were come down, prayed for them, that they might receive the Holy Ghost: 16 (For as yet he was fallen upon none of them: only they were baptized in the name of the Lord Jesus.) 17 Then laid they their hands on them, and they received the Holy Ghost.

**Acts 10:44-46 (KJV)**

44 While Peter yet spake these words, the Holy Ghost fell on all them which heard the word. 45 And they of the circumcision which believed were astonished, as many as came with Peter, because that on the Gentiles also was poured out the gift of the Holy Ghost. 46 For they heard them speak with tongues, and magnify God. Then answered Peter,

**Acts 11:14-16 (KJV)**
14 Who shall tell thee words, whereby thou and all thy house shall be saved. 15 And as I began to speak, the Holy Ghost fell on them, as on us at the beginning. 16 Then remembered I the word of the Lord, how that he said, John indeed baptized with water; but ye shall be baptized with the Holy Ghost.

**Acts 15:7-9 (KJV)**
7 And when there had been much disputing, Peter rose up, and said unto them, Men and brethren, ye know how that a good while ago God made choice among us, that the Gentiles by my mouth should hear the word of the gospel, and believe. 8 And God, which knoweth the hearts, bare them witness, giving them the Holy Ghost, even as he did unto us; 9 And put no difference between us and them, purifying their hearts by faith.

With the baptism in the Holy Spirit come such experiences as:

an overflowing fullness of the Spirit,

**John 7:37-39 (KJV)**
37 In the last day, that great day of the feast, Jesus stood and cried, saying, If any man thirst, let him come unto me, and drink. 38 He that believeth on me, as the scripture hath said, out of his belly shall flow rivers of living water. 39 (But this spake he of the Spirit, which they that believe on him should receive: for the Holy Ghost was not yet given; because that Jesus was not yet glorified.)

**Acts 4:8 (KJV)**
8 Then Peter, filled with the Holy Ghost, said unto them, Ye rulers of the people, and elders of Israel,

a deepened reverence for God,

**Acts 2:43 (KJV)**
43 And fear came upon every soul: and many wonders and signs were done by the apostles.

**Hebrews 12:28 (KJV)**
28 Wherefore we receiving a kingdom which cannot be moved, let us have grace, whereby we may serve God acceptably with reverence and godly fear:

an intensified consecration to God and dedication to His work,

**Acts 2:42 (KJV)**

42 And they continued stedfastly in the apostles' doctrine and fellowship, and in breaking of bread, and in prayers.

and, a more active love for Christ, for His Word and for the lost,

**Mark 16:20 (KJV)**

20 And they went forth, and preached everywhere, the Lord working with them, and confirming the word with signs following. Amen.

# CHAPTER 24
# THE INITIAL PHYSICAL EVIDENCE OF THE BAPTISM IN THE HOLY SPIRIT

The baptism of believers in the Holy Spirit is witnessed by the initial physical sign of speaking with other tongues as the Spirit of God gives them utterance.

**Acts 2:4 (KJV)**
4 And they were all filled with the Holy Ghost, and began to speak with other tongues, as the Spirit gave them utterance.

The speaking in tongues in this instance is the same in essence as the gift of tongues, but is different in purpose and use.

**1 Corinthians 12:4-10 (KJV)**
4 Now there are diversities of gifts, but the same Spirit. 5 And
there are differences of administrations, but the same Lord. 6 And
there are diversities of operations, but it is the same God which
worketh all in all. 7 But the manifestation of the Spirit is given to
every man to profit withal. 8 For to one is given by the Spirit the
word of wisdom; to another the word of knowledge by the same
Spirit; 9 To another faith by the same Spirit; to another the gifts of
healing by the same Spirit; 10 To another the working of miracles; to
another prophecy; to another discerning of spirits; to another divers
kinds of tongues; to another the interpretation of tongues:

**1 Corinthians 12:28 (KJV)**

28 And God hath set some in the church, first apostles, secondarily prophets, thirdly teachers, after that miracles, then gifts of healings, helps, governments, diversities of tongues.

If you have not received the Baptism of The Holy Spirit, with the evidence of Speaking in Tongues, I would ask you to pray about receiving this wonderful gift from God.

# CHAPTER 25
# THE WORK OF THE HOLY SPIRIT

To fully understand the significance and implication of the work of the Holy Spirit, we must first remember that the Holy Spirit is the third part of the Trinity of God; and, as such, the Holy Spirit is very much God. The Bible teaches us that there is one God, who reveals Himself to us in three persons, God the Father, God the Son, and, God the Holy Spirit.

The works of the Holy Spirit are described in both the Old Testament and the New Testament:

**The Holy Spirit Shared in Creation**

The Holy Spirit is part of the Trinity at the time of creation and played a part in creation. In Genesis 1:2-3, when the earth had been created but was in darkness and without form, the Spirit of God "was hovering over its surface." Then God said, "Let there be light," and light was created. (NLT)

**The Holy Spirit Raised Jesus from the Dead**

In Romans 8:11, written by the Apostle Paul, he says, "The Spirit of God, who raised Jesus from the dead, lives in you. And just as he raised Christ from the dead, he will give life to your mortal body by this same Spirit living within you." (NLT) The Holy Spirit is given the physical application of the salvation and redemption provided by God the Father on the basis of the sacrifice of God the Son.

**The Holy Spirit Places Believers into Christ's Body**

Paul also writes in 1 Corinthians 12:13, "For we were all baptized by one Spirit into one body, whether Jews or Greeks, slave or free, and we were all given the one Spirit to drink." (NIV)

As in the Romans passage, the Holy Spirit dwells in believers following salvation, and this unites them in spiritual communion. An illustration of the Holy Spirit's indwelling is stated also in John 3:5 where Jesus says that no one can enter the kingdom of God unless he is born of water and the Spirit.

**The Holy Spirit Proceeds from the Father and from Christ**

In two passages in the Gospel according to John, Jesus speaks of the Holy Spirit being sent from the Father and from Christ. Jesus calls the Holy Spirit the Counselor. In John 15:26: [Jesus speaking] says, "When the Counselor comes, whom I will send to you from the Father, the Spirit of truth who goes out from the Father, he will testify about me." (NIV) In John 16:7: [Jesus speaking] says, "But I tell you the truth: It is for your good that I am going away. Unless I go away, the Counselor will not come to you; but if I go, I will send him to you." (NIV)

As the Counselor, the Holy Spirit guides the believer, including making the believer aware of sins they have committed.

**The Holy Spirit Gives Divine Gifts**

The divine gifts that the Holy Spirit gave to the disciples at Pentecost can also be given to other believers for the common good, although they may receive different gifts. The Spirit decides which gift to give each person, as the Apostle Paul writes in 1 Corinthians 12:7-11 there are many gifts: Wisdom, Knowledge, Healing, Miraculous powers, Prophecy, Distinguishing between spirits, Speaking in different kinds of tongues, Interpretation of tongues.

Also found in the New Testament are gifts of Administration/ Ruling, Evangelism, Exhortation, Faith, Giving, Helps/Serving/ Ministering, Mercy, Teaching, and others

**The Holy Spirit convicts,** He comforts, He reveals, He redeems, and so much more.

I would encourage you this week to spend some time with your Bible helps books, or other references, to investigate more of the work of the Holy Spirit. He is God, working in us, and through us, to accomplish the will of our Heavenly Father.

# CHAPTER 26
## THE DOMINANT SPIRIT

In Genesis chapters one and two, we are told that God created human beings (male and female) on the sixth day of creation. Scripture informs us that God created us to have a body, soul, and spirit. With the body we have "world-consciousness" through our senses of sight, smell, taste, touch, and hearing. With our soul we have "self-consciousness" through our mind, will, emotions, and intellect. With our spirit we have "God-consciousness"; for it is through the spirit of man that we have connectivity with the Holy Spirit of God, Who guides, directs, and instructs, our daily path.

In the previous chapter, we recognized that God is a Triune of Father, Son, and Holy Spirit. A triune cannot be separated or broken. When God created man, He created us as a tripartite of body, soul, and spirit. A tripartite can be separated, and, in time will be separated.

Briefly, it is my personal belief, and interpretation of the Bible, that one day (should the Lord tarry, and the rapture has not taken place yet) our deceased body will be laid to rest in a grave. At that point, for the Christian, our spirit (God-consciousness) will live on and be ushered into the presence of God (to the thief on the cross Jesus said "This day you will be with me in paradise." Luke 23:43) The soul will cease to exist at that point for the Christian (there will no longer be a need for self-consciousness.) For the unsaved person, at death, their body and soul will rest in the grave, awaiting the Great White Throne Judgement, at which time they will be cast into the Lake of Fire for eternity. (The soul of that person will give a self-consciousness of the anguish of hell, but there will be no more God-consciousness. I believe the lack of God-consciousness will be a form of hell, in and of itself.)

At the time of our salvation, when the Holy Spirit came to

dwell with us, He came to direct our path in the way that would be pleasing to God. To that end, the Apostle Paul wrote to the church in Galatia, "I am crucified with Christ: nevertheless I live; yet not I, but Christ liveth in me: and the life which I now live in the flesh I live by the faith of the Son of God, who loved me, and gave himself for me." Galatians 2:20

In other words, my soul (mind, will, emotions, and intellect) are no longer to direct my path and actions. I am no longer living for what I want to do, but it is Christ (through the indwelling of the Holy Spirit) who is now wanting to guide and direct my daily activities.

Said another way, the spirit of man, who is in constant communion and fellowship with God through the Holy Spirit, should now be the dominant part of me, as a Christian.

The conscious life of a Christian can only receive and submit to God's guidance when the Holy Spirit, through man's spirit (God-consciousness), dominates it.

Paul writes that we are to "…lay aside the old self…and… be renewed in the spirit of your mind." Ephesians 4:22 & 23. By laying aside our old self, we are to lay aside our governance by our soul (self-consciousness), and "be renewed in the spirit…" (our God-consciousness).

In Romans 8:6 Paul writes, "For the mind set on the flesh is death, but the mind set on the Spirit is life and peace…". "The mind set on the flesh" is having our soul directing us… and that brings spiritual death to a person. However, "the mind set on the Spirit…" is having the direction of the Holy Spirit (notice the capital "S"), through the fellowship with our spirit (small "s"), which brings us life (Spiritual life) and peace.

The objective this week is to understand that although we are created with a body, soul, and spirit, our spirit and soul must be divided, and dominance given to the spirit, for our direction to be received from the Holy Spirit.

Feeding on God's Word (which we will cover in Chapters 30 - 32) will enable us to have the faith to yield our life and desires to be dominated by the Holy Spirit.

Colossians 3:9 & 10 says, "…you laid aside the old self with its evil practices, and have put on the new self who is being renewed to a true knowledge according to the image of the One who created him."

This week, let's do the same thing and "lay aside our old self", and strive more to be renewed by the Holy Spirit, Whose breath was breathed into us at creation.

# CHAPTER 27
## THE SPIRITUAL WAR

Naturally, when we were looking at last week's study on The Dominant Spirit, we certainly had to recognize that wanting our spirit to have dominion over our soul is really much more difficult than what it sounds like on paper. To that end, this week we will address the spiritual warfare that we can expect to arise… "expect" being the operative word here.

Obviously our enemy, Satan, does not want our God-conscious spirit to be dominant within us. He would prefer that we would continue to let our self-conscious soul direct our actions, because our mind, will, emotions, and intellect are inferior to that of an omnipotent, omniscient, God.

So, let's start off this week by understanding John's words, found in 1 John 4:4 "… greater is he that is in you, than he that is in the world."

Last week we acknowledged that God dwells within us through His Holy Spirit, so what John is writing is that the Holy Spirit that dwells within the Christian is greater that anyone and anything that is in the world. The inference here is that of the spirit of antichrist, which John mentioned earlier in 1 John 4, by every demon, demonic power, and Satan himself.

God is greater than Satan or any of his minions, and God is dwelling in us! That should be sufficient, and we should be able to end this chapter right here, but let's go on a little further and look at a few of the ways that Satan would try to bully his way into our minds. (Remember from last week, our mind is part of our soul, which is to be subservient to our dominant spirit.)

So, how does Satan try to persuade us to not obey God, through the leading of the Holy Spirit? Let's make a list:

**Temptation**

**James 1:13-15 (KJV)**
13 Let no man say when he is tempted, I am tempted of God: for God cannot be tempted with evil, neither tempteth he any man:
14 But every man is tempted, when he is drawn away of his own lust, and enticed. 15 Then when lust hath conceived, it bringeth forth sin: and sin, when it is finished, bringeth forth death.

Satan will try to tempt us with other things he believes our mind, will, emotions and intellect would prefer, over what God desires for us.

**Opposition**

Paul, writing to the church in Thessaloniki says,
**1 Thessalonians 2:18 (KJV)**
" Wherefore we would have come unto you, even I Paul, once and again; but Satan hindered us."

Satan "hindered" him from doing what he believed was God's will. Can you remember hindrances in your own life that precluded you from doing what you thought you should do?

**Deception**

**2 Corinthians 11:14-15 (NLT) tells us:**
14 But I am not surprised! Even Satan disguises himself as an angel of light. 15 So it is no wonder that his servants also disguise themselves as servants of righteousness. In the end they will get the punishment their wicked deeds deserve.

Satan and his demons will disguise themselves as righteousness, and try to convince us that what they are suggesting is really God's idea. Thankfully, the Holy Spirit dwelling within us will reveal their deception, and lead us into the truth.

**Oppression**

**Revelation 2:10 (NLT)**
"Don't be afraid of what you are about to suffer. The devil will throw some of you into prison to test you. You will suffer for ten days. But if you remain faithful even when facing death, I will give you the crown of life."

If you would like to see an illustration of Satanic oppression, read the story of Joseph, in the Book of Genesis, as he journeyed from his dream to his destiny. Hold fast!

This week, here is how we can win The Spiritual War:

**Ephesians 6:10-17 (NLT)**
10 A final word: Be strong in the Lord and in his mighty power.
11 Put on all of God's armor so that you will be able to stand firm
against all strategies of the devil. 12 For we are not fighting against
flesh-and-blood enemies, but against evil rulers and authorities of
the unseen world, against mighty powers in this dark world, and
against evil spirits in the heavenly places. 13 Therefore, put on every
piece of God's armor so you will be able to resist the enemy in the
time of evil. Then after the battle you will still be standing firm. 14
Stand your ground, putting on the belt of truth and the body armor of
God's righteousness. 15 For shoes, put on the peace that comes from
the Good News so that you will be fully prepared. 16 In addition to
all of these, hold up the shield of faith to stop the fiery arrows of the
devil. 17 Put on salvation as your helmet, and take the sword of the
Spirit, which is the word of God.

Let's clothe our self with the armor of God, and face our enemy as the loser we know he is, because we have already overcome him, through the shed blood of Jesus Christ at Calvary.

Also, this week, remember:

Ro. 8:37 says, "You are more than a conqueror", that's the King James.

"You are the undisputed champion", that's the Ray James.

# CHAPTER 28
## FACTORING IN OUR HUMANITY

Let's continue a little further with the thought of Spiritual Warfare. Last week we primarily considered Satan's role in the battle, so this week let's look at our human position regarding this battle.

The bottom line to this week's study is: you must be serious, and have a deep desire to want to please God in all that you do and say. You must have a deep desire to want to please God, and be obedient to what He desires of you. Without a serious desire to live a spiritual, Christ-like life, you will never fully understand the life that God desires for you to have.

We often try to fool ourselves into thinking it's easy to trust in God, and it's easy to do what is right, and it's easy to follow the prompting of the Holy Spirit. However, I would suggest it really isn't. Of course, that doesn't give us a license to quit trying.

Consider with me the Apostle Paul's struggle with sin. A man who was beaten, whipped, and thrown into prison. A real hero of the faith. A Christian without sin… or was he? Read his own account of his struggles:

**Romans 7:14-24 (NLT)**

14 So the trouble is not with the law, for it is spiritual and
good. The trouble is with me, for I am all too human, a slave to
sin. 15 I don't really understand myself, for I want to do what is
right, but I don't do it. Instead, I do what I hate. 16 But if I know

that what I am doing is wrong, this shows that I agree that the law is good. 17 So I am not the one doing wrong; it is sin living in me that does it. 18 And I know that nothing good lives in me, that is, in my sinful nature. I want to do what is right, but I can't. 19 I want to do what is good, but I don't. I don't want to do what is wrong, but I do it anyway. 20 But if I do what I don't want to do, I am not really the one doing wrong; it is sin living in me that does it. 21 I have discovered this principle of life—that when I want to do what is right, I inevitably do what is wrong. 22 I love God's law with all my heart. 23 But there is another power within me that is at war with my mind. This power makes me a slave to the sin that is still within me. 24 Oh, what a miserable person I am! Who will free me from this life that is dominated by sin and death?

Kind of wants to make you take Paul down off the pedestal, doesn't it?

What a struggle he was having; and it doesn't appear as if it was a one-time event. It sounds like it was a daily struggle that he had trying to follow the voice of God… trying to follow the leading of the Holy Spirit; doesn't it?

Listen to his words:

"The trouble is with me."
"I'm all too human."
"I'm a slave to sin."
"I want to do what is right, but I don't do it."
"Instead I do what I hate." (He's using strong words. "Slave." "Hate".)

In verses 18 and 19 he begins to repeat himself… I'm sure out of frustration.

In verse 22 he admits he loves God's law with all of his heart. (But that's not enough.)

In verse 23 he finally hits the nail on the head when he says, "there is another power within me that is at war with my mind. This power makes me a slave to the sin that is still within me".

That's another strong word: Power. Where? In his mind. There it is again: in his mind!

But notice verse 24, this time in the King James Version: 24 O wretched man that I am! who shall deliver me from the body of this death?

There was a practice during Paul's days, that when a person had committed a crime that was punishable by death, the prisoner would be chained to another person who was either hours from dying, or already dead. The Apostle Paul recognizes his condition of dying. Not physically, but spiritually. He recognizes he cannot continue this way, and that he must do better.

Let's turn the page to chapter 8 and finish his story:

**Romans 8 (KJV)**

1 There is therefore now no condemnation to them which are in Christ Jesus, who walk not after the flesh, but after the Spirit.
2 For the law of the Spirit of life in Christ Jesus hath made me free from the law of sin and death. 3 For what the law could not do, in that it was weak through the flesh, God sending his own Son in the likeness of sinful flesh, and for sin, condemned sin in the flesh:
4 That the righteousness of the law might be fulfilled in us, who walk not after the flesh, but after the Spirit. 5 For they that are after the flesh do mind the things of the flesh; but they that are after the Spirit the things of the Spirit. 6 For to be carnally minded is death; but to be spiritually minded is life and peace. 7 Because the carnal mind is enmity against God: for it is not subject to the law of God, neither indeed can be. 8 So then they that are in the flesh cannot please God. 9 But ye are not in the flesh, but in the Spirit, if so be that the Spirit of God dwell in you. Now if any man have not the Spirit of Christ, he is none of his. 10 And if Christ be in you, the body is dead because of sin; but the Spirit is life because of righteousness. 11 But if the Spirit of him that raised up Jesus from the dead dwell in you, he that raised up Christ from the dead shall also quicken your mortal bodies by his Spirit that dwelleth in you.

Two verses, real quick:

Verse 2: "For the law of the Spirit of life in Christ Jesus hath made me free from the law of sin and death."

The law of the Spirit of life in Christ Jesus... Capital "S". The Holy Spirit hath made me free...free! Released from Satan's grip and, Verse 11: But if the Spirit (capital "S" again) of him that raised up Jesus from the dead dwell in you... The Holy Spirit. God, the Spirit... raised Jesus from the dead..."he... shall also quicken your mortal bodies by his Spirit that dwelleth in you."

Thought for this week: If you are struggling to follow the direction of the Holy Spirit, cheer up, you're in good company; so did the Apostle Paul, and so does everyone else. So don't give up, you MUST press on until you know that you know that you know that the Holy Spirit of God that raised up Jesus Christ from (physical) death, will also raise you up from your (spiritual) death and you WILL overcome our enemy, Satan, and you will be victorious... if you don't quit.

# CHAPTER 29
## SANCTIFICATION

Sanctification is an act of separation from that which is evil, and of dedication unto God.

**Romans 12:1-2 (KJV)**
1 I beseech you therefore, brethren, by the mercies of God, that ye present your bodies a living sacrifice, holy, acceptable unto God, which is your reasonable service. 2 And be not conformed to this world: but be ye transformed by the renewing of your mind, that ye may prove what is that good, and acceptable, and perfect, will of God.

**1 Thessalonians 5:23 (KJV)**
23 And the very God of peace sanctify you wholly; and I pray God your whole spirit and soul and body be preserved blameless unto the coming of our Lord Jesus Christ.

**Hebrews 13:12 (KJV)**
12 Wherefore Jesus also, that he might sanctify the people with his own blood, suffered without the gate.

The Scriptures teach a life of "holiness without which no man shall see the Lord."

**Hebrews 12:14 (KJV)**
14 Follow peace with all men, and holiness, without which no man shall see the Lord:

By the power of the Holy Spirit we are able to obey the command: "Be ye holy, for I am holy."

**1 Peter 1:15-16 (KJV)**

15 But as he which hath called you is holy, so be ye holy in all manner of conversation; 16 Because it is written, Be ye holy; for I am holy.

Sanctification is realized in the believer by recognizing his identification with Christ in His death and resurrection, and by faith reckoning daily upon the fact of that union, and by offering every faculty continually to the dominion of the Holy Spirit.

**Romans 6:1-11 (KJV)**

1What shall we say then? Shall we continue in sin, that grace may abound? 2 God forbid. How shall we, that are dead to sin, live any longer therein? 3 Know ye not, that so many of us as were baptized into Jesus Christ were baptized into his death? 4 Therefore we are buried with him by baptism into death: that like as Christ was raised up from the dead by the glory of the Father, even so we also should walk in newness of life. 5 For if we have been planted together in the likeness of his death, we shall be also in the likeness of his resurrection: 6 Knowing this, that our old man is crucified with him, that the body of sin might be destroyed, that henceforth we should not serve sin. 7 For he that is dead is freed from sin. 8 Now if we be dead with Christ, we believe that we shall also live with him: 9 Knowing that Christ being raised from the dead dieth no more; death hath no more dominion over him. 10 For in that he died, he died unto sin once: but in that he liveth, he liveth unto God. 11 Likewise reckon ye also yourselves to be dead indeed unto sin, but alive unto God through Jesus Christ our Lord.

**Romans 6:13 (KJV)**

13 Neither yield ye your members as instruments of unrighteousness unto sin: but yield yourselves unto God, as those that are alive from the dead, and your members as instruments of righteousncss unto God.

**Romans 8:1-2 (KJV)**

1 There is therefore now no condemnation to them which are in Christ Jesus, who walk not after the flesh, but after the Spirit. 2 For the law of the Spirit of life in Christ Jesus hath made me free from the law of sin and death.

**Romans 8:13 (KJV)**

13 For if ye live after the flesh, ye shall die: but if ye through the Spirit do mortify the deeds of the body, ye shall live.

**Galatians 2:20 (KJV)**

20 I am crucified with Christ: nevertheless I live; yet not I, but Christ liveth in me: and the life which I now live in the flesh I live by the faith of the Son of God, who loved me, and gave himself for me.

**Philippians 2:12-13 (KJV)**

12 Wherefore, my beloved, as ye have always obeyed, not as in my presence only, but now much more in my absence, work out your own salvation with fear and trembling. 13 For it is God which worketh in you both to will and to do of his good pleasure.

**1 Peter 1:5 (KJV)**

5 Who are kept by the power of God through faith unto salvation ready to be revealed in the last time.

# CHAPTER 30
## THE BIBLE - GOD'S WORD

Without a doubt the Bible is the most important book ever written, and the most read book ever written. The history and events of the Bible are continuously being confirmed through excavations, and through the discovery of other manuscripts. It is a literary masterpiece. Ethics, civilizations, and morals have been patterned from it.

The Old Testament contained, is the New Testament explained.

However, the Bible is not just a masterpiece of literature, or merely a book of ethics and morals…

**The Bible is the God-inspired, infallible Word of God**

Another incredible fact about the Bible is that it was written over a period of approximately 1,500 years by 40 +/- human authors, as they were inspired of God.

**2 Timothy 3:16-17** says,
"All scripture is given by inspiration of God, and is profitable for doctrine, for reproof, for correction, for instruction in righteousness: 17 That the man of God may be perfect, thoroughly furnished unto all good works."

Now, watch this. The word translated from the Greek into the English for "inspiration", is the same word that is translated from the Hebrew into English found in Genesis 2:7 for the word "breathed".
**Genesis 2:7 (KJV)**

7 And the Lord God formed man of the dust of the ground, and breathed into his nostrils the breath of life; and man became a living soul.

In other words, the words of the Bible were "breathed" into the spirits and minds of the authors, by the Holy Spirit of God.

There is one central theme found throughout the 66 books of the Bible… Salvation. Moreover, there is one central character found through its pages… Jesus Christ, the Son of God.

The Old Testament introduces us to the sin of man, and the need for a savior, and predicts the advent of the Messiah; and, the New Testament introduces us to the birth of the Messiah, Jesus.

The Bible, God's Word, is a compilation of everything that God wants us to know about living a life that is pleasing to Him, through a personal and intimate relationship with Him. So, why do the surveys today, of Christians, reveal that the majority of these Christians have never, or do not, read the Bible from cover to cover.

There is a Spiritual answer to every situation and circumstance that we face today that is addressed in God's Word. Why don't Christians want God's answers to the issues they face today?

Jesus even informed us of the necessity of reading His Word:

**Matthew 4:4 (KJV)**

4 "…It is written, Man shall not live by bread alone, but by every word that proceedeth out of the mouth of God."

Please understand, you cannot be an effective disciple, discipler, or disciple-maker, if you are not reading the Word of God.

Here's what Jesus said about it:

**John 8:31 (KJV)**

31 "Then said Jesus to those Jews which believed on him, If ye continue in my word, then are ye my disciples indeed;"

We must "continue" in His Word. Not just a casual one-time glance at it. Continue.

In 2 Timothy 3:16 (above) Paul tells us God's Word is good for doctrine, for reproof, for correction, for instruction in righteousness. Who doesn't need that?

In just ten minutes a day, you can read the entire Bible in one year. Reading ten chapters a day you can read the entire Bible in 18 weeks. Who doesn't have 10 minutes a day?

Mix it up. Read from different translations. I have 29 translations in my library. www.biblegateway.com has over 60 translations and versions, and it seems like new versions are constantly coming out.

This week find a new version of the Bible that is easy to read… and start reading, or, start reading it again, or, continue reading.

# CHAPTER 31
## DEEPER INTO GOD'S WORD

Last week we considered how incredibly important it is to read, and study, the Bible, - - the Word of God.

To help with your reading, and studying the Word of God, this week I want to make a few suggestions:

1. Find a translation, or version of the Bible that is easy for you to read. There are several versions of the Bible from the original language. The King James Version was based on a manuscript that earlier translators had used. Later Bibles like the Revised Standard Version used manuscripts with noticeable differences in the original language, and these became bigger differences upon translation.

Very briefly, here is the difference between a translation, a revision, a paraphrase, and a version:

Translation - exactly what it says, the Bible version is the result of translation from another language.

Revision - a translation that relies on a reference Bible version for wording (when the translation agrees with the reference version).

Paraphrase - a story in which every paragraph tells you what a paragraph in the Bible says or means.

Version - any Bible that is significantly different from all other Bibles. Translations, revisions and paraphrases are all examples of versions.

The discovery of the Dead Sea Scrolls and other manuscripts from time to time is generally the reason to make any of these changes, noted above. I only address this because there is sometimes confusion as to why we have so many translations or versions of the Bible, and I believe a student of the Bible should have some knowledge of this.

2. Remember that the Bible really does mean what it says. To better understand this, make a mental note as to the time the passage you are reading was written. What was the culture of that day? What were the events or history setting? Also, ask yourself whether this passage is literal or symbolic. Generally, this should be obvious. If you are unsure, possibly a commentary or other Bible reference book will add insight into this matter.

3. Use Bible study reference books. There are many Bible reference books available today: encyclopedias, dictionaries, commentaries, and word-study books. I find the Strong's Concordance especially useful for word-study help. One additional thought… I (personally) don't like to use books that are written by a single author, because you only receive that one person's thoughts on the subject. Rather, many reference books have several contributors, which help to get a more balanced interpretation of a collective thought on a particular subject.

4. Also, try not to skip around and just read one or two verses at a time. In order to gain a full understanding of the passage, you may need to start reading many verses before, or even a chapter or more before the verse(s) you are trying to understand, to put that verse into better context.

5. Don't think you need to understand everything you read. Let scripture interpret scripture. Remember, the Old Testament contained, is the New Testament explained. After reading the Bible from cover to cover over one hundred times, I will promise you will still understand more the next time you read it, than you did before.

6. Keep a journal of what you are reading, and make notes of words, phrases, and events that you would like to go back and study in further depth. I guarantee your journal will get filled-up quickly.

Bible study groups are an excellent way to read the Bible. It gives you an opportunity to hear what others are thinking as they read a chapter, and gives you the shared experience from someone who may have previously studied that passage in more detail.

Above all else, when you sit to read your Bible, begin with

a prayer to the author of the Word. Ask God to speak to you with a fresh breath of understanding, to give you clarity of mind, and understanding. God wants you to understand His Word; that is why He gave it to us.

Be blessed this week as you read your Bible, whether it is your very first time, or your two hundredth time.

# CHAPTER 32
## HOW CRITICAL IS THE WORD OF GOD

As previously stated, the Bible is a compilation of everything that God wants to say to us. Let me rephrase that, the Creator of heaven and earth has chosen to communicate with us through His Word, the Bible. How critical it is for us to understand what He wants to say to us through His Word. Yet, I routinely speak to Christians who tell me they have never read the Bible.

In Chapter 26, we considered the necessity of the Christian having a "dominant spirit". Our spirit gives us God-consciousness, and God's Word informs us of His desire to communicate with us, on a deeper, personal, intimate level.

The Spirit of God, Who inspired the authors of the Bible, will speak to us as we read His Word, to give us understanding of what God is saying to us personally. Let me illustrate that another way. Sometimes we will read a passage of Scripture, and we will glean an understanding that God is saying one thing to us. Another person can read the same passage of Scripture and garner an entirely different understanding. Then, later, we may read the same verses and gain even another interpretation.

We are reading the same scripture, but our interpretation is changing because the circumstances in our life, has changed; and/or our spiritual maturity has grown.

My dad and I were talking about safety, and at the end of the conversation, dad told me to go clean my room. I'm guessing he doesn't want me to trip on something and get hurt. A week later dad and I are talking about air-borne germs that are causing people to get sick because of coming into contact with the germs. At the end of the conversation, dad again asks me to go clean my room. My interpretation this time is that the surfaces need to be sanitized, so I don't get sick. Both times dad simply said, "go clean your room"; but my interpretation was different each time.

That is another reason why it is so critical for us to pray before reading the Bible. We need to prepare our soul (self-awareness) and our spirit (God-awareness) to hear what God wants to say to us. But that is only two-thirds of who we are. What about our body? Will our bodies be affected by God's Word? Absolutely!

After God speaks to us, through His Word, we then take our understanding of what He has said to us into the world around us. When the Holy Spirit directs our self-awareness and our God-awareness, the activities of our body should reflect our new understanding.

Let me illustrate this fact through God's Word:

**Romans 6: 12 – 13**

"Therefore do not let sin reign in your mortal body that you should obey its lusts, and do not go on presenting the members of your body as instruments of unrighteousness; but present yourselves to God as those alive from the dead, and your members as instruments of righteousness to God."

What does that mean? How can our newly convicted-of sin, from reading God's Word, reign in our body? Well, maybe we are now convicted of gossiping (tongue), looking and lusting for something (eyes), desiring to steal something (hands), listening to a vulgar joke (ears), and the list could go on and on.

In the above Scripture, being "alive from the dead" is being brought to spiritual life, from the dead (lifelessness) spiritual understanding of what God is speaking to us through His Word.

So our body is used to manifest the Holy Spirit's life, and dominance, in us. Galatians 5:22-25 shows us how:

**Galatians 5:22-25**

22 But the fruit of the Spirit is love, joy, peace, longsuffering, gentleness, goodness, faith, 23 Meekness, temperance: against such there is no law. 24 And they that are Christ's have crucified the flesh with the affections and lusts. 25 If we live in the Spirit, let us also walk in the Spirit.

The Fruit of the (Holy) Spirit, is dwelling within our spirit, controlling our soul (mind, will, emotions, and intellect), and is revealed through our bodies, daily.

Here is how the Bible describes it:

**Galatians 5:16-17 (KJV)**
16 This I say then, Walk in the Spirit, and ye shall not fulfil the lust of the flesh. 17 For the flesh lusteth against the Spirit, and the Spirit against the flesh: and these are contrary the one to the other: so that ye cannot do the things that ye would.

The fruit of the Spirit is in direct opposition to our souls. Go back and read Romans 7:14-24, from Chapter 28 again, to help reinforce this understanding.

This week, pay particular attention to how your body, soul, and spirit all work in conjunction and in harmony with each other, to glorify God, in all you do and say.

# CHAPTER 33
## PRAYER

If you were to ask someone to define prayer, they would probably tell you that prayer is when you tell God about all the things you have need of (healing in your body, money to pay a bill, a parking spot close to the Mall entrance, and so forth.)

But prayer is so much more. Hebrews 4:16 says:

**Hebrews 4:16**

16 Let us therefore come boldly unto the throne of grace, that we may obtain mercy, and find grace to help in time of need.

What is the throne of grace? It is the place where we enter into God's manifold presence, in this world of His omnipresence. In other words, God is everywhere, but when I approach Him in prayer, I humble myself before Him, and He meets me where I am.

Paul wrote in Philippians 4:6-7, that we can bring our cares to God:

**Philippians 4:6-7**

6 Be careful for nothing; but in every thing by prayer and supplication with thanksgiving let your requests be made known unto God. 7 And the peace of God, which passeth all understanding, shall keep your hearts and minds through Christ Jesus.

Permit me to unpack that a little. Supplication in prayer is an earnest and humble pleading. We are to earnestly and humbly ask God for His provision of what we have need of, and do it with a grateful heart, that we know He loves us, and desires His best for us. With that understanding, there is a supernatural peace that fills us, which we cannot describe. I still have the need, but I know God is in control, and I know He will do what is best (Romans 8:28), and I will simply trust Him to accomplish His will for me. Paul wraps up verse 7 by saying God "shall keep your hearts and minds through Christ Jesus." Or, said another way, He will keep our "spirit" and our "soul" at peace through His Son, Jesus Christ. (In other words, everything will be okay.)

In addition to our talking to God, we also need to allow time in prayer for God to talk to us.

Prayer is having a conversation with God, and, just like any other conversation, it requires both listening and talking.

It is critically important that we listen to what God is saying to us. Sometimes He may be saying He doesn't want to do things the way we are asking, that He has another plan. Maybe He will just ask us to trust Him for a future answer. We need to hear what God is saying, by His speaking into our spirits, or, possibly, what He has already said, through His Word, the Bible.

Just as Jesus is often recorded in the Bible as praying alone, with His Father, so should we be in the habit of often praying with our heavenly Father.

**1 Thessalonians 5:17** (KJV) says we are to "Pray without ceasing." The word "ceasing" in the original Greek (adialĕiptōs) means uninterruptedly. In other words, get rid of all distractions, and find a secluded place where no one will disturb you, and have a conversation with God.

**Matthew 6:6 (NLT)** says, "But when you pray, go away by yourself, shut the door behind you, and pray to your Father in private. Then your Father, who sees everything, will reward you."

There are also times when corporate prayer with others is appropriate, in a church service, or in a small group. You will find many occasions in the Book of Acts when the disciples, and others prayed togcthcr.

Just as conversation strengthens the relationships between people (husband and wife, parents and children, employers and employees, doctors and patients, and so forth), so does prayer (conversation) strengthen the relationship between us, and God. God desires to have a personal relationship with us, and we should equally desire to have a personal relationship with Him.

Our conversations with God are crucial to our fellowship with Him (see Chapter 20).

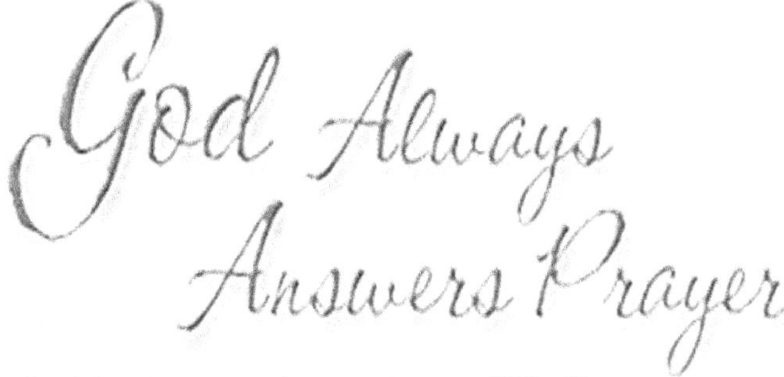


**When the idea is not right, God says, "No."**

No - when the idea is not the best.

No - when the idea is absolutely wrong.

No - when though it may help you, it could create problems for someone else.

**When the time is not right, God says, "Slow."**

What a catastrophe it would be if God answered every prayer at the snap of your fingers. Do you know what would happen? God would become your servant, not your master. Suddenly God would be working for you instead of you working for God. Remember: God's delays are not God's denials. God's timing is perfect. Patience is what we need in prayer.

**When you are not right, God says, "Grow."**

The selfish person has to grow in unselfishness.

The cautious person must grow in courage.

The timid person must grow in confidence.

The dominating person must grow in sensitivity.

The critical person must grow in tolerance.

The negative person must grow in positive attitudes.

The pleasure-seeking person must grow in compassion for suffering people.

**When everything is all right, God says, "Go."**

Then miracles happen:

...A hopeless alcoholic is set free!

....A drug addict finds release!

....A doubter becomes as a child in his belief.

....Diseased tissue responds to treatment, and healing begins.

....The door to your dream suddenly swings open and there stands God saying, "Go!"

My mother's favorite song was, In the Garden. Here are the lyrics:

I come to the garden alone
While the dew is still on roses
And the voice I hear falling
On my ear the son of God discloses

And He walks with me and He talks with me
And He tells me I am His own
And the joy we share as we tarry there
None other has ever known

He speaks and the sound of His voice
Is so sweet the birds hush their singing
And the melody that He gave to me
Within my heart is ringing

And He walks with me and He talks with me
And He tells me I am His own
And the joy we share as we tarry there
None other has ever known

This week, get alone with God, and have a sweet conversation with Him. He will love it.

# CHAPTER 34
# THE CHURCH AND ITS MISSION (PART ONE)

The Church is the Body of Christ, the habitation of God through the Spirit, with divine appointments for the fulfillment of the great commission. Each believer, born of the Spirit, is an integral part of the General Assembly and Church of the Firstborn, which are written in heaven.

**Ephesians 1:22-23 (KJV)**
22 And hath put all things under his feet, and gave him to be
the head over all things to the church, 23 Which is his body, the
fulness of him that filleth all in all.

**Ephesians 2:22 (KJV)**
22 In whom ye also are builded together for an habitation of God through the Spirit.

**Hebrews 12:23 (KJV)**
23 To the general assembly and church of the firstborn, which are written in heaven, and to God the Judge of all, and to the spirits of just men made perfect,

Since God's purpose concerning man is to seek and to save that which is lost, to be worshipped by man, to build a body of believers in the image of His Son, and to demonstrate His love and compassion for all the world, the priority reason for our being as part of the Church is:

1. To be an agency of God for evangelizing the world.

**Acts 1:8 (KJV)**
8 But ye shall receive power, after that the Holy Ghost is come upon you: and ye shall be witnesses unto me both in Jerusalem, and in all Judaea, and in Samaria, and unto the uttermost part of the earth.

**Matthew 28:19-20 (KJV)**
19 Go ye therefore, and teach all nations, baptizing them in the name of the Father, and of the Son, and of the Holy Ghost: 20 Teaching them to observe all things whatsoever I have commanded you: and, lo, I am with you always, even unto the end of the world. Amen.

**Mark 16:15-16 (KJV)**
15 And he said unto them, Go ye into all the world, and preach the gospel to every creature. 16 He that believeth and is baptized shall be saved; but he that believeth not shall be damned.

2. To be a corporate body in which man may worship God.

**1 Corinthians 12:13 (KJV)**
13 For by one Spirit are we all baptized into one body, whether we be Jews or Gentiles, whether we be bond or free; and have been all made to drink into one Spirit.

3. To be a channel of God's purpose to build a body of saints being perfected in the image of His Son.

**Ephesians 4:11-16 (KJV)**
11 And he gave some, apostles; and some, prophets; and some, evangelists; and some, pastors and teachers; 12 For the perfecting of the saints, for the work of the ministry, for the edifying of the body of Christ: 13 Till we all come in the unity of the faith, and of the knowledge of the Son of God, unto a perfect man, unto the measure of the stature of the fulness of Christ: 14 That we henceforth be no more children, tossed to and fro, and carried about with every wind of doctrine, by the sleight of men, and cunning craftiness, whereby they lie in wait to deceive; 15 But speaking the truth in love, may grow up into him in all things, which is the head, even Christ: 16 From whom the whole body fitly joined together and compacted by that which every joint supplieth, according to the effectual working in the measure of every part, maketh increase of the body

unto the edifying of itself in love.

**1 Corinthians 12:28 (KJV)**
28 And God hath set some in the church, first apostles, secondarily prophets, thirdly teachers, after that miracles, then gifts of healings, helps, governments, diversities of tongues.

**1 Corinthians 14:12 (KJV)**
12 Even so ye, forasmuch as ye are zealous of spiritual gifts, seek that ye may excel to the edifying of the church.

4. To be a people who demonstrate God's love and compassion for all the world.

**Psalm 112:9 (KJV)**
9 He hath dispersed, he hath given to the poor; his righteousness endureth for ever; his horn shall be exalted with honour.

**Galatians 2:10 (KJV)**
10 Only they would that we should remember the poor; the same which I also was forward to do.

**James 1:27 (KJV)**
27 Pure religion and undefiled before God and the Father is this, To visit the fatherless and widows in their affliction, and to keep himself unspotted from the world.

Are you beginning to see the church is more than the brick and mortar building that you go to on Sundays?

# CHAPTER 35
## THE CHURCH AND ITS MISSION (PART TWO)

We exist expressly to give continuing emphasis to this reason for being in the New Testament apostolic pattern by teaching and encouraging believers to be baptized in the Holy Spirit. This experience:

1. Enables them to evangelize in the power of the Spirit with accompanying supernatural signs.

**Mark 16:15-20 (KJV)**

15 And he said unto them, Go ye into all the world, and preach
the gospel to every creature.16 He that believeth and is baptized
shall be saved; but he that believeth not shall be damned. 17 And
these signs shall follow them that believe; In my name shall they
cast out devils; they shall speak with new tongues; 18 They shall
take up serpents; and if they drink any deadly thing, it shall not hurt
them; they shall lay hands on the sick, and they shall recover. 19
So then after the Lord had spoken unto them, he was received up
into heaven, and sat on the right hand of God. 20 And they went
forth, and preached every where, the Lord working with them, and
confirming the word with signs following. Amen.

**Acts 4:29-31 (KJV)**

29 And now, Lord, behold their threatenings: and grant unto thy servants, that with all boldness they may speak thy word,

30 By stretching forth thine hand to heal; and that signs and

wonders may be done by the name of thy holy child Jesus. 31 And when they had prayed, the place was shaken where they were assembled together; and they were all filled with the Holy Ghost, and they spake the word of God with boldness.

**Hebrews 2:3-4 (KJV)**

3 How shall we escape, if we neglect so great salvation; which at the first began to be spoken by the Lord, and was confirmed unto us by them that heard him; 4 God also bearing them witness, both with signs and wonders, and with divers miracles, and gifts of the Holy Ghost, according to his own will?

2. Adds a necessary dimension to worshipful relationship with God.

**1 Corinthians 2:10-16 (KJV)**

10 But God hath revealed them unto us by his Spirit: for the Spirit searcheth all things, yea, the deep things of God. 11 For what man knoweth the things of a man, save the spirit of man which is in him? even so the things of God knoweth no man, but the Spirit of God. 12 Now we have received, not the spirit of the world, but the spirit which is of God; that we might know the things that are freely given to us of God. 13 Which things also we speak, not in the words which man's wisdom teacheth, but which the Holy Ghost teacheth; comparing spiritual things with spiritual. 14 But the natural man receiveth not the things of the Spirit of God: for they are foolishness unto him: neither can he know them, because they are spiritually discerned. 15 But he that is spiritual judgeth all things, yet he himself is judged of no man. 16 For who hath known the mind of the Lord, that he may instruct him? but we have the mind of Christ.

**1 Corinthians 12 (KJV)**

12 Now concerning spiritual gifts, brethren, I would not have you ignorant.

**1 Corinthians 12:2-31 (KJV)**

2 Ye know that ye were Gentiles, carried away unto these dumb idols, even as ye were led. 3 Wherefore I give you to understand, that no man speaking by the Spirit of God calleth Jesus accursed: and that no man can say that Jesus is the Lord, but by the Holy Ghost. 4 Now there are diversities of gifts, but the same Spirit. 5 And there are differences of administrations, but the same Lord. 6 And there are diversities of operations, but it is the same God which worketh all in all.7 But the manifestation of the Spirit is given to

every man to profit withal. 8 For to one is given by the Spirit the word of wisdom; to another the word of knowledge by the same Spirit; 9 To another faith by the same Spirit; to another the gifts of healing by the same Spirit; 10 To another the working of miracles; to another prophecy; to another discerning of spirits; to another divers kinds of tongues; to another the interpretation of tongues: 11 But all these worketh that one and the selfsame Spirit, dividing to every man severally as he will. 12 For as the body is one, and hath many members, and all the members of that one body, being many, are one body: so also is Christ. 13 For by one Spirit are we all baptized into one body, whether we be Jews or Gentiles, whether we be bond or free; and have been all made to drink into one Spirit. 14 For the body is not one member, but many. 15 If the foot shall say, Because I am not the hand, I am not of the body; is it therefore not of the body? 16 And if the ear shall say, Because I am not the eye, I am not of the body; is it therefore not of the body? 17 If the whole body were an eye, where were the hearing? If the whole were hearing, where were the smelling? 18 But now hath God set the members every one of them in the body, as it hath pleased him. 19 And if they were all one member, where were the body? 20 But now are they many members, yet but one body. 21 And the eye cannot say unto the hand, I have no need of thee: nor again the head to the feet, I have no need of you.22 Nay, much more those members of the body, which seem to be more feeble, are necessary: 23 And those members of the body, which we think to be less honourable, upon these we bestow more abundant honour; and our uncomely parts have more abundant comeliness. 24 For our comely parts have no need: but God hath tempered the body together, having given more abundant honour to that part which lacked. 25 That there should be no schism in the body; but that the members should have the same care one for another. 26 And whether one member suffer, all the members suffer with it; or one member be honoured, all the members rejoice with it. 27 Now ye are the body of Christ, and members in particular. 28 And God hath set some in the church, first apostles, secondarily prophets, thirdly teachers, after that miracles, then gifts of healings, helps, governments, diversities of tongues. 29 Are all apostles? are all prophets? are all teachers? are all workers of miracles? 30 Have all the gifts of healing? do all speak with tongues? do all interpret? 31 But covet earnestly the best gifts: and yet shew I unto you a more excellent way.

# CHAPTER 36
# THE CHURCH AND ITS MISSION (PART THREE)

**1 Corinthians 13 (KJV)**

1Though I speak with the tongues of men and of angels, and have not charity, I am become as sounding brass, or a tinkling cymbal. 2 And though I have the gift of prophecy, and understand all mysteries, and all knowledge; and though I have all faith, so that I could remove mountains, and have not charity, I am nothing. 3 And though I bestow all my goods to feed the poor, and though I give my body to be burned, and have not charity, it profiteth me nothing. 4 Charity suffereth long, and is kind; charity envieth not; charity vaunteth not itself, is not puffed up, 5 Doth not behave itself unseemly, seeketh not her own, is not easily provoked, thinketh no evil; 6 Rejoiceth not in iniquity, but rejoiceth in the truth; Beareth all things, believeth all things, hopeth all things, endureth all things. 8 Charity never faileth: but whether there be prophecies, they shall fail; whether there be tongues, they shall cease; whether there be knowledge, it shall vanish away. 9 For we know in part, and we prophesy in part. 10 But when that which is perfect is come, then that which is in part shall be done away. 11 When I was a child, I spake as a child, I understood as a child, I thought as a child: but when I became a man, I put away childish things. 12 For now we see through a glass, darkly; but then face to face: now I know in part; but then shall I know even as also I am known. 13 And now abideth faith, hope, charity, these three; but the greatest of these is charity.

**1 Corinthians 14 (KJV)**

1Follow after charity, and desire spiritual gifts, but rather that ye may prophesy. 2 For he that speaketh in an unknown tongue speaketh not unto men, but unto God: for no man understandeth him; howbeit in the spirit he speaketh mysteries. 3 But he that prophesieth speaketh unto men to edification, and exhortation, and comfort. 4 He that speaketh in an unknown tongue edifieth himself; but he that prophesieth edifieth the church. 5 I would that ye all spake with tongues but rather that ye prophesied: for greater is he that prophesieth than he that speaketh with tongues, except he interpret, that the church may receive edifying. 6 Now, brethren, if I come unto you speaking with tongues, what shall I profit you, except I shall speak to you either by revelation, or by knowledge, or by prophesying, or by doctrine? 7 And even things without life giving sound, whether pipe or harp, except they give a distinction in the sounds, how shall it be known what is piped or harped? 8 For if the trumpet give an uncertain sound, who shall prepare himself to the battle? 9 So likewise ye, except ye utter by the tongue words easy to be understood, how shall it be known what is spoken? for ye shall speak into the air. 10 There are, it may be, so many kinds of voices in the world, and none of them is without signification. 11 Therefore if I know not the meaning of the voice, I shall be unto him that speaketh a barbarian, and he that speaketh shall be a barbarian unto me.12 Even so ye, forasmuch as ye are zealous of spiritual gifts, seek that ye may excel to the edifying of the church. 13 Wherefore let him that speaketh in an unknown tongue pray that he may interpret.14 For if I pray in an unknown tongue, my spirit prayeth, but my understanding is unfruitful.15 What is it then? I will pray with the spirit, and I will pray with the understanding also: I will sing with the spirit, and I will sing with the understanding also.

16 Else when thou shalt bless with the spirit, how shall he hat occupieth the room of the unlearned say Amen at thy giving of thanks, seeing he understandeth not what thou sayest? 17 For thou verily givest thanks well, but the other is not edified. 18 I thank my God, I speak with tongues more than ye all: 19 Yet in the church I had rather speak five words with my understanding, that by my voice I might teach others also, than ten thousand words in an unknown tongue. 20 Brethren, be not children in understanding: howbeit in malice be ye children, but in understanding be men. 21 In the law it is written, With men of other tongues and other lips will I speak unto this people; and yet for all that will they not hear me, saith the Lord. 22 Wherefore tongues are for a sign, not to them that believe, but to them that believe not: but prophesying serveth not for them that believe not, but for them which believe. 23 If therefore the whole

church be come together into one place, and all speak with tongues, and there come in those that are unlearned, or unbelievers, will they not say that ye are mad? 24 But if all prophesy, and there come in one that believeth not, or one unlearned, he is convinced of all, he is judged of all: 25 And thus are the secrets of his heart made manifest; and so falling down on his face he will worship God, and report that God is in you of a truth. 26 How is it then, brethren? when ye come together, every one of you hath a psalm, hath a doctrine, hath a tongue, hath a revelation, hath an interpretation. Let all things be done unto edifying. 27 If any man speak in an unknown tongue, let it be by two, or at the most by three, and that by course; and let one interpret. 28 But if there be no interpreter, let him keep silence in the church; and let him speak to himself, and to God. 29 Let the prophets speak two or three, and let the other judge. 30 If any thing be revealed to another that sitteth by, let the first hold his peace. 31 For ye may all prophesy one by one, that all may learn, and all may be comforted. 32 And the spirits of the prophets are subject to the prophets. 33 For God is not the author of confusion, but of peace, as in all churches of the saints. 34 Let your women keep silence in the churches: for it is not permitted unto them to speak; but they are commanded to be under obedience as also saith the law. 35 And if they will learn any thing, let them ask their husbands at home: for it is a shame for women to speak in the church. 36 What? came the word of God out from you? or came it unto you only? 37 If any man think himself to be a prophet, or spiritual, let him acknowledge that the things that I write unto you are the commandments of the Lord. 38 But if any man be ignorant, let him be ignorant. 39 Wherefore, brethren, covet to prophesy, and forbid not to speak with tongues 40 Let all things be done decently and in order.

# CHAPTER 37
# THE CHURCH AND ITS MISSION (PART FOUR)

3. Enables them to respond to the full working of the Holy Spirit in expression of fruit and gifts and ministries as in New Testament times for the edifying of the body of Christ and care for the poor and needy of the world.

**Galatians 5:22-26 (KJV)**
22 But the fruit of the Spirit is love, joy, peace, longsuffering,
gentleness, goodness, faith, 23 Meekness, temperance: against such
there is no law. 24 And they that are Christ's have crucified the flesh
with the affections and lusts. 25 If we live in the Spirit, let us also
walk in the Spirit. 26 Let us not be desirous of vain glory, provoking
one another, envying one another.

**Matthew 25:37-40 (KJV)**
37 Then shall the righteous answer him, saying, Lord, when
saw we thee an hungred, and fed thee? or thirsty, and gave thee
drink? 38 When saw we thee a stranger, and took thee in? or naked,
and clothed thee? 39 Or when saw we thee sick, or in prison, and
came unto thee? 40 And the King shall answer and say unto them,
Verily I say unto you, Inasmuch as ye have done it unto one of the
least of these my brethren, ye have done it unto me.

**Galatians 6:10 (KJV)**
10 As we have therefore opportunity, let us do good unto all men, especially unto them who are of the household of faith.

**1 Corinthians 14:12 (KJV)**

12 Even so ye, forasmuch as ye are zealous of spiritual gifts, seek that ye may excel to the edifying of the church.

**Ephesians 4:11-12 (KJV)**

11 And he gave some, apostles; and some, prophets; and some, evangelists; and some, pastors and teachers; 12 For the perfecting of the saints, for the work of the ministry, for the edifying of the body of Christ:

**1 Corinthians 12:28 (KJV)**

28 And God hath set some in the church, first apostles, secondarily prophets, thirdly teachers, after that miracles, then gifts of healings, helps, governments, diversities of tongues.

**Colossians 1:29 (KJV)**

29 Whereunto I also labour, striving according to his working, which worketh in me mightily.

As you can see, by studying the last four weeks, there is much more to the ministry of the church, through its mission, than just having a service or two every week.

This week, pray about how God can use you in the ministry of your church, and, then, make an appointment with your pastor to explore the opportunities that may be available to you.

# CHAPTER 38
## THE MINISTRY

A divinely called and scripturally ordained ministry has been provided by our Lord for the fourfold purpose of leading the Church in:

Evangelization of the world,

**Mark 16:15-20 (KJV)**
15 And he said unto them, Go ye into all the world, and preach
the gospel to every creature. 16 He that believeth and is baptized
shall be saved; but he that believeth not shall be damned. 17 And
these signs shall follow them that believe; In my name shall they
cast out devils; they shall speak with new tongues; 18 They shall
take up serpents; and if they drink any deadly thing, it shall not hurt
them; they shall lay hands on the sick, and they shall recover. 19
So then after the Lord had spoken unto them, he was received up
into heaven, and sat on the right hand of God. 20 And they went
forth, and preached every where, the Lord working with them, and
confirming the word with signs following. Amen.

Worship of God,

**John 4:23-24 (KJV)**
23 But the hour cometh, and now is, when the true worshippers
shall worship the Father in spirit and in truth: for the Father seeketh
such to worship him. 24 God is a Spirit: and they that worship him
must worship him in spirit and in truth.

Building a body of saints being perfected in the image of His Son,

**Ephesians 4:11-16 (KJV)**
11 And he gave some, apostles; and some, prophets; and some, evangelists; and some, pastors and teachers; 12 For the perfecting of the saints, for the work of the ministry, for the edifying of the body of Christ: 13 Till we all come in the unity of the faith, and of the knowledge of the Son of God, unto a perfect man, unto the measure of the stature of the fulness of Christ: 14 That we henceforth be no more children, tossed to and fro, and carried about with every wind of doctrine, by the sleight of men, and cunning craftiness, whereby they lie in wait to deceive; 15 But speaking the truth in love, may grow up into him in all things, which is the head, even Christ:
16 From whom the whole body fitly joined together and compacted by that which every joint supplieth, according to the effectual working in the measure of every part, maketh increase of the body unto the edifying of itself in love.

Meeting human need with ministries of love and compassion,

**Psalm 112:9 (KJV)**
9 He hath dispersed, he hath given to the poor; his righteousness endureth for ever; his horn shall be exalted with honour.

**Galatians 2:10 (KJV)**
10 Only they would that we should remember the poor; the same which I also was forward to do.

**James 1:27 (KJV)**
27 Pure religion and undefiled before God and the Father is this, To visit the fatherless and widows in their affliction, and to keep himself unspotted from the world.

Let me hasten to add: ministry is not just the pastor's duty, it is the duty of every child of God.

Ask yourself this week, what ministry has God called you to?

# CHAPTER 39
## DIVINE HEALING

Divine healing is an integral part of the gospel. Deliverance from sickness is provided for in the atonement, and is the privilege of all believers.

**Isaiah 53:4-5 (KJV)**
4 Surely he hath borne our griefs, and carried our sorrows: yet we did esteem him stricken, smitten of God, and afflicted. 5 But he was wounded for our transgressions, he was bruised for our iniquities: the chastisement of our peace was upon him; and with his stripes we are healed.

**Matthew 8:16-17 (KJV)**
16 When the even was come, they brought unto him many that were possessed with devils: and he cast out the spirits with his word, and healed all that were sick: 17 That it might be fulfilled which was spoken by Esaias the prophet, saying, Himself took our infirmities, and bare our sicknesses.

**James 5:14-16 (KJV)**
14 Is any sick among you? let him call for the elders of the church; and let them pray over him, anointing him with oil in the name of the Lord: 15 And the prayer of faith shall save the sick, and the Lord shall raise him up; and if he have committed sins, they shall be forgiven him. 16 Confess your faults one to another, and pray one for another, that ye may be healed. The effectual fervent prayer of a righteous man availeth much.

*I need to pause here for comment. It has been said, by many, that healing was for "those" days, but not for today. That simply is not true. There are testimonies of documented healings and miracles nearly every day.*

*My own healing is one of those "modern day" stories. Long story short, I was born unable to speak. The doctors had no idea if it was physiological or psychological; nevertheless, I could not talk. Schools in the District of Columbia refused to enroll me for first grade, because of my condition, and the same was true of schools in Virginia. (This was long before Special Education was available.)*

*My unchurched parents took me to a "faith evangelist", who prayed the prayer of faith, and I was instantaneously healed. So much so, that I stood up in the back seat of our 1955 baby-blue BelAir Chevrolet and talked all the way home, from North Carolina to Washington, DC; and no one had the nerve to tell me to shut up and sit down.*

*I once gave that testimony at a crusade in Guadalajara, Mexico and a woman came to me after the service and asked if the same God Who gave me speech, could give her sight. The woman appeared to me to be about 146 years old, and I assumed she was stricken with cataracts or glaucoma. We prayed the prayer of faith, and her sight was given. I asked the interpreter to ask her when she lost her sight, and what had happened. Later he informed me that she told him she was born blind, and that night she was seeing God's creation for the very first time. Praise God! (Incidentally, the woman was only in her 70's)*

*If you have come to tell me healing is not for today, you've come too late.*

*Disciples, followers of The Great Physician, need to understand healing is for today!*

# CHAPTER 40
## THE BLESSED HOPE

The resurrection of those who have fallen asleep in Christ and their translation together with those who are alive and remain unto the coming of the Lord is the imminent and blessed hope of the church.

**1 Thessalonians 4:16-17 (KJV)**
16 For the Lord himself shall descend from heaven with a shout, with the voice of the archangel, and with the trump of God:
and the dead in Christ shall rise first: 17 Then we which are alive
and remain shall be caught up together with them in the clouds, to meet the Lord in the air: and so shall we ever be with the Lord.

**Romans 8:23 (KJV)**
23 And not only they, but ourselves also, which have the first fruits of the Spirit, even we ourselves groan within ourselves, waiting for the adoption, to wit, the redemption of our body.

**Titus 2:13 (KJV)**
13 Looking for that blessed hope, and the glorious appearing of the great God and our Saviour Jesus Christ;

**1 Corinthians 15:51-52 (KJV)**
51 Behold, I shew you a mystery; We shall not all sleep, but
we shall all be changed, 52 In a moment, in the twinkling of an eye,
at the last trump: for the trumpet shall sound, and the dead shall be raised incorruptible, and we shall be changed.

*As I am writing this, Easter is less than two weeks away, and, I am reminded of the question: Why did Jesus fold the napkin that covered His face in the tomb.*

*The Gospel of John (20:7) tells us that the napkin, which was placed over the face of Jesus, was not just thrown aside like His grave clothes.*

*The Bible tells us that the napkin was neatly folded, and was placed at the head of that stony coffin.*

*Early Sunday morning, while it was still dark, Mary Magdalene came to the tomb and found that the stone had been rolled away from the entrance. (I would encourage you to read this entire story in John's gospel.)*

*It was Simon Peter who went inside the tomb, and noticed the linen napkin neatly folded, and lying to the side.*

*The significance of that folded napkin is found in a dinner-time practice of that day. The servant would wait for the master of the house to finish eating, before clearing the table. When the master was finished, he would rise from the table, wipe his fingers, his mouth, clean his beard, and would wad up the napkin and toss it on the table. The servant would then know to clear the table.*

*If the master got up from the table, folded his napkin, and laid it beside his plate, the servant would know not to clean the table; because the master was coming back.*

*The folded napkin meant, "I'm coming back".*

*My friend, please understand, Our Master is coming back! That is the Blessed Hope of the church today.*

This week we looked at the Rapture of the Church. Over the next few weeks I want to use Scripture to describe some of the events that will follow the Rapture. Please notice we will be looking at what the Bible says, and not considering the current events as we interpret the coming of our Lord. We will be looking at the facts of the Bible, and not conjecture by human opinions.

My format for the next few weeks will be to answer the who, what, when, where, why, and how questions of the end-time events, as appropriate.

# CHAPTER 41
## THE RAPTURE OF THE CHURCH & OUR NEW GLORIFIED BODY

1. The Rapture of the Church

Even though the word "rapture" is never used in the Bible, the event of the calling away of the saints to heaven is described. Also, please remember the Rapture of the Church and the Second Coming are two separate events.

Last week we looked at several scriptures pertaining to the Rapture, so I will not repeat them.

Those who will be involved in the Rapture will be:

a. Jesus Christ, Who gave Himself for the church, His bride.
b. The archangel, mentioned in 1 Thess. 4:16, whom I personally believe will be Michael, because of his scriptural involvement in the end-time prophecy of Daniel 12 and Jude 9.
c. Every Christian who has already died (1 Thess. 4:16, and 1 Co. 15:52)
d. Every Christian who is still living at the time of the Rapture (1 Thess. 4:17)
e. And, every child who has not reached the age of accountability; (those too young to make an intelligent decision to follow Christ, or not to follow Him); and all those who are mentally incapable of making the decision.

When the Rapture will take place has been the topic of many

discussions and debates. Although the Bible does not stipulate whether it will be pre-tribulation, mid-tribulation, or post-tribulation, the Bible does state the Great Tribulation will be a period of God pouring out His wrath upon the world, and the Bible states God's people are not appointed to God's wrath. Therefore, I subscribe to the idea of a pre-tribulation rapture. (I also believe some of the typologies and symbolisms of the Bible support my decision. Moreover, the fact that after the Rapture of the church, the church is not mentioned in the Bible being here on earth.)

What will be the results of the Rapture?

a. All Christians, babies, small children, and mentally challenged people will be gone, and
b. There will be a time of havoc on the earth as never before seen.

2. Our New Glorified Body

At the time of the Christian's salvation, their soul changed, and their spirit changed, but their body stayed the same, adaptable to this three-dimensional world.

The Bible does not give us complete information about our New Glorified Body, but it does have a few things to say about it. We know:

a. Our new body will be like the body of Christ. (Philippians 3:20-21 & 1 John 3:2)
b. Our new body will be a body of flesh and bones. (Luke 24:39 and Job 19:25-26)
c. Our new body will be recognizable. (1 Corinthians 13:12 & 1 Co. 15:35-44)
d. Our new body will be a spirit-dominated body. (1 Co. 15:44 & Mark 14:38)
e. Our new body will be unlimited by time, space, energy, and matter. (Luke 24:31, John 20:19 and John 20:26)
f. Our body will be an eternal body. (2 Corinthians 5:1 & 2 Thess. 4:17 ["ever"] )
g. Our body will be a glorious body. (1 Co. 15:43, Romans 8:18, Daniel 12:2-3)

The aging process that began in the Garden of Eden will be eliminated. Terminated forever.

We will have no pain, no suffering, no pills, no need for surgeries, no glasses, no hearing aids, no false teeth, no pacemakers… it will be glorious.

This week, contemplate on how wonderful the New Glorified Body of the Christians caught up in the Rapture will be; and then ask yourself the question:  why wouldn't everyone want to be a Christian?

# CHAPTER 42
# THE JUDGMENT SEAT OF CHRIST, & THE MARRIAGE SUPPER OF THE LAMB

1. The Judgment Seat of Christ.

This event will immediately follow the rapture of the church in heaven, and, it is the judgment where all believers will stand before Jesus and give an account for their stewardship. (Ro. 14: 10-12, 1 Co. 3:11-15, & 2 Co. 5:10)

Note, the phrase "Judgment Seat" actually comes from the Greek word "Bema" which was commonly used during that time, and, was a raised platform in the arenas, where the athletes and Olympians stood to receive their rewards (after judged for their performance). Jesus Christ will be the Judge (John 5:22 & Acts 10:42).

Jesus will not be concerned with punishing the believers for sin. Their sin has already been covered by His blood, at the cross of Calvary, when they repented of it. However, He will be concerned with how Christians conducted themselves regarding their stewardship while on earth. (1 Peter 4:10 & 1 Co. 4:1-2) The results of this Judgment is that some will suffer loss (1 Co. 3:15), some will not receive every reward Christ had stored for them (2 John 8) and, some will receive the reward(s) for what they have done (1 Co. 3:14).

Five rewards the Bible talks about are:

a. An Incorruptible Crown (1 Co. 9:24-27)
b. A Crown of Rejoicing (1 Thess. 2:18 & 20)

c. The Crown of Life (Revelation 2:10)
d. The Crown of Righteousness (2 Timothy 4:6-8) and,
e. A Crown of Glory (1 Peter 5:2-4)

Knowing that every Christian will give an account of their lives (obedience & disobedience) one day, before Christ, should make them want to live every day pleasing to God. (1 John 2:28)

2. The Marriage & Marriage Supper of the Lamb

Jesus Christ is the Lamb, and the Groom. The church, the Christian, is the Bride.

I imagine the pattern of the marriage will probably follow the pattern of the typical New Testament wedding;

a. The Betrothal Stage (selection & promise of marriage)
   (1) The Christians have been chosen (Ephesians 1:3-4)
   (2) The payment, with His own blood (1 Co. 6:19-20)
   (3) The dowry was given (1 Peter 1:18-19)

b. The Presentation of the Bride (Jude 24 & 2 Co. 11:2)

c. The Celebration. The public Marriage Supper (Luke 2:37)

The Judgment Seat of Christ will be a very solemn time, and, I believe, many tears will be shed as we recognize the gravity of what is happening, and, for many, their unpreparedness.

Conversely, the Marriage, and the Marriage Supper of the Lamb will be an awesome celebration as we are joined with our Groom, the Lord Jesus Christ, never to be separated again.

In the view of a pre-tribulation rapture, please recognize that while the church is in heaven at the Judgment Seat of Christ, and the Marriage, and Marriage Supper of the Lamb, the unsaved will still remain on earth, and will be going through the events of the Great Tribulation.

The Great Tribulation will be the topic of the next two week's study, followed by a study on the Second Coming of Christ at the end of chapter 44.

# CHAPTER 43
## THE GREAT TRIBULATION

Remember, we have already concluded, for this study, that immediately following the Rapture of the Church, the Great Tribulation period will begin on earth. Also, remember, the Great Tribulation is still during the Age/Dispensation of Grace (salvation of the unbeliever will still be possible).

1. So there is no confusion while reading the Bible, it is also good to note the Great Tribulation is also called by other names/ titles:

a. The Tribulation (Matthew 24:21 & 29)
b. The Time of Trouble (Daniel 12:1)
c. The Overspreading of Abominations (Daniel 9:27)
d. The Indignation (Isaiah 26:20 & 34:2)
e. The Hour of His Judgment (Revelation 14:6-7)
f. The Great Day of His Wrath (Revelation 6:17)
g. The Time of the End (Daniel 12:9)
h. The Seventieth Week (Daniel 9:24-27)
i. The Great Day of The Lord (Joel 2:11 & Zephaniah 1:14)
j. The Time of Jacob's Trouble (Jeremiah 30:7)
k. The Day of God's Vengeance (Isaiah 34:8 & 63:4)

The Great Tribulation is referred to by many titles, and, by the events of those titles.

Some believe the title, "The End of the World", found in Matthew 13:40 & 49 also refers to the Great Tribulation, but I believe this refers to the Judgment of the Nations (the Parable of the Sheep & Goats.) Please feel free to make your own decision, there is much debate on this.

For the purpose of this study, we will simply use the title, The Great Tribulation.

2. Let's next review the Purpose of the Great Tribulation. (We must believe there is a reason for everything God does.)

a. To prepare Israel for her Messiah (Primarily). (Ezekiel 20:37-38, & Zechariah 13:8-9)

b. It will be a time to pour out Judgments on the Unrighteous. (Romans 1:18 & 2 Thessalonians 2:8-12) The delusion spoken of here will be (among other lies) the reason for the disappearance of millions of people. (Then, Isaiah 26:20-21)

3. Thirdly, the Mark of the Tribulation, which is, of course, 666. (Revelation 13:16-18)

(1) In Scriptural numerology, the number 6, is the number of man.

(2) This Mark will be required to buy/sale/trade during the Great Tribulation.

(3) This number will invoke God's wrath. (Revelation 16:1-2)

(4) The Mark will seal a person's future. (Revelation14: 9-11)

4. The 144,000 of the Great Tribulation. (Revelation 7:1-4)

(1) They are Jews, from the 12 tribes of Israel.

(2) They are servants of God. (Revelation 7:3)

(3) They are specifically selected of God for a particular purpose. (Revelation 14:1-4)

(4) They will preach, "Endure to the end" and then Christ will return. (The Second Coming).

5. The 2 Witnesses of the Great Tribulation (Revelation 11:3)

(1) These 2 Witnesses will have a very special power. (Revelation 11:5-6)

(2) They will be the "light of Christ" on the earth. ("Candlesticks")

(3) They will have a limited time. (Revelation 11:7)

(4) They will receive no further respect. (Revelation (11:8-10) (No respect because of the deception of Satan.)

(5) But they will have a big surprise for their scoffers. (Revelation 11:11-12)

Next week, Chapter 44, we will continue with #6. The Action of the Great Tribulation.

I realize this is a very vague outline of the Great Tribulation, and looking over my hundreds of pages of notes, there is much left out. My intention is to show there is much to be accomplished during the seven years of the Great Tribulation. You will not be able to grasp it all in a two week discipleship study; but I trust you will take time to study this further.

# CHAPTER 44
## THE GREAT TRIBULATION, & THE SECOND COMING OF CHRIST

By now I'm sure you will agree that hundreds of pages could be written on the Great Tribulation; and, in fact, many books have been written on this event. Nevertheless, my intent is just to give an overview of it. Let's continue:

6. The Action of the Great Tribulation

Although many things happen simultaneously, we will attempt to look at the actions of the Great Tribulation chronologically, as much as possible.

The primary action of the Great Tribulation will be the opening of the seals, sounding of the trumpets, and the pouring of the vials (bowls), found in the Book of Revelation.

1. The opening of the seals:
    a. The Anti-Christ will appear on a white horse (Revelation 6:1-2)
    b. The appearance of a red horse… War (Revelation 6:3-4)
    c. The appearance of a black horse… Hunger (Revelation 6:5-6)
    d. The appearance of a pale horse… Famine & Disease (Revelation 6:7-8)
    e. The martyrs are revealed, whose souls are crying out. (Revelation 6:9-11)

f. Physical calamities upon the earth. (Revelation 6:12-17)
g. Silence in heaven. The 7th Seal containing the 7 trumpets. (Revelation 8:1)

2. The blowing of the trumpets:

a. One-third of the earth set on fire. (Revelation 8:7)
b. One-third of the sea-water becomes blood (Revelation 8:8-9)
c. One-third of the fresh-water turns bitter. (Revelation 8:10-11)
d. Light is cut off for eight hours. (Revelation 8:12-13)
e. Demon-possessed locust torment people. (Revelation 9:1-6)
f. Four demons are released from the Euphrates River (Revelation 9:13-19)
g. An earthquake & hailstorm proclaim Christ's soon return. (Revelation 11:15-19)

3. The pouring of the vials (bowls):

a. Cancerous boils. (Revelation 16:1-2)
b. Everything remaining in the sea dies. (Revelation 16:3)
c. All remaining fresh-water is contaminated. (Revelation 16:4)
d. Everyone is burned by the Sun's heat. (Revelation 16:8-9)
e. The Kingdom of the Beast is plunged into darkness. (Revelation 16:10-11)
f. Demonic spirits gather armies to go to Armageddon (Revelation 16:12-16)
g. Islands disappear & mountains are leveled. (Revelation 16:17-21)

During the time of the Great Tribulation I believe well over a billion people will die horrific deaths caused by the seal/trumpet/vial catastrophes to those who have taken the Mark of the Beast; and then our Lord returns at The Second Coming of Christ.

The Second Coming of Christ is when Jesus Christ will physically return to earth, and this Coming will be a "bridge" between the Great Tribulation and the Millennial Reign of Christ.

Jesus will not be coming this second time to be denied or

crucified. He will be coming as the King of Kings and the Lord of Lords, to establish His divine rule and reign over all of His creation; and the armies of heaven, His church, His bride, will follow Him.

Just before establishing His divine rule and reign over the earth, Jesus will:

a. Deliver the Jews
b. Defeat the armies at Armageddon
c. Judge the Nations, and
d. Judge the Fallen Angels

I believe Daniel 12:11-12 tells us specifically, that these events can certainly be accomplished during this 45-day transitional period that Daniel is describing.

If for no other reason, I trust Chapters 43 and 44 will help us to understand yet another reason to ensure we are ready to meet our Lord and Savior when the trumpet sounds, for the Rapture of the Church. You will NOT want to go through the Great Tribulation here on earth.

# CHAPTER 45
# THE MILLENNIAL REIGN OF CHRIST (PART ONE)

There is an enormous amount of Scripture regarding the Millennial Reign, and, again, we will not be able to cover all of it in this brief discipleship study.

Remember, the Second Coming, that we have just studied, is the bridge between the worst time (Great Tribulation) and the best time (Millennial Reign), this earth has ever known.

During the Great Tribulation, people (Jews and Gentiles alike) have suffered greatly, and the entire planet has suffered greatly… destruction by wars, famines, catastrophic diseases, earthquakes, huge hail, fire, mountains crumbled, fresh water and salt water contaminated, and, it appears, by the effects of biological, chemical, and nuclear warfare.

To say the earth has been totally destroyed, would be an understatement. So, what will the Millennial Reign be like?

1. What will the Millennial Reign be like for Satan?
    a. Satan will be chained in the Bottomless Pit, shut up and sealed, not allowed to deceive anyone for the thousand years of the Millennial Reign. (Revelation 20:1-3)

2. What will the Millennial Reign be like for our Savior, Jesus Christ?
    a. This is the time, as the King of Kings, and Lord of Lords, that Jesus will rule the earth.

b. He will ensure it is a time of peace. (Isaiah 2:4, & 2:17-18, and Ezekiel 34:25)
c. Jesus will restore the agricultural condition of the earth. (Isiah 2:4 & Micah 4:3)
d. Jesus will ensure comfort is provided for everyone. (Isaiah 12:1 & 51:3)
e. Jesus will ensure perfect justice is administered (Isaiah 9:7)
f. Jesus will ensure there is no sickness or disease. (Isaiah 29:17-19 & 65:20)
g. Jesus will ensure proper instructions are given. (Jeremiah 3:14-15 & Micah 4:2)

3. What will the Millennial Reign be like for the Saints?
   a. We will be forever with the Lord. (1 Thessalonians 4:17)
   b. The things which applied to Jesus, will also apply (affect) us. We will assist Him. (Revelation 20:4-6)
   c. We will continue to forever worship God. (Isaiah 66:23 & Zechariah 14:16)

4. What will the Millennial Reign be like for the survivors of the Great Tribulation, who will enter this period in their natural, physical, bodies?
   a. They will continue to reproduce. (Ezekiel 47:22-23)
   b. They will suffer punishment (for disobedience). (Jeremiah 30:20 & Isaiah 66:22-24)
   c. They will labor. (Isaiah 6:21-23)
   d. They will be prosperous. (Ezekiel 36:29 & 38)
   e. They all will speak one language (Zephaniah 3:9)

5. What will the Millennial Reign be like for the salvage earth?
   a. The earth will be restored. (Amos 9:13)
   b. Animal life will be changed. (Isaiah 11:6-9)

6. What will the Millennial Reign be like for saved Israel?
   a. They will be restored to their first relationship to God. (Isaiah 62:2-5)
   b. Israel will be exalted before the Gentiles. (Isaiah 62:2)
   c. Israel will become God's witness during the Millennial Reign. (Zephaniah 3:20)

7. What will the Millennial Reign be like for the Sanctuary?
    a. The temple will again be present. (Isaiah 2:3)
    b. Sacrifices will again take place. (Isaiah 56:5-7)

# CHAPTER 46
# THE MILLENNIAL REIGN OF CHRIST (PART TWO)

The second coming of Christ is the visible return of Christ with His saints to reign on earth for one thousand years.

**Zechariah 14:5 (KJV)**
5 And ye shall flee to the valley of the mountains; for the valley of the mountains shall reach unto Azal: yea, ye shall flee, like as ye fled from before the earthquake in the days of Uzziah king of Judah: and the Lord my God shall come, and all the saints with thee.

**Matthew 24:27 (KJV)**
27 For as the lightning cometh out of the east, and shineth even unto the west; so shall also the coming of the Son of man be.

**Matthew 24:30 (KJV)**
30 And then shall appear the sign of the Son of man in heaven: and then shall all the tribes of the earth mourn, and they shall see the Son of man coming in the clouds of heaven with power and great glory.

**Revelation 1:7 (KJV)**
7 Behold, he cometh with clouds; and every eye shall see him, and they also which pierced him: and all kindreds of the earth shall wail because of him. Even so, Amen.

**Revelation 19:11-14 (KJV)**

11 And I saw heaven opened, and behold a white horse; and he that sat upon him was called Faithful and True, and in righteousness he doth judge and make war. 12 His eyes were as a flame of fire, and on his head were many crowns; and he had a name written, that no man knew, but he himself. 13 And he was clothed with a vesture dipped in blood: and his name is called The Word of God. 14 And the armies which were in heaven followed him upon white horses, clothed in fine linen, white and clean.

**Revelation 20:1-6 (KJV)**

1And I saw an angel come down from heaven, having the key of the bottomless pit and a great chain in his hand. 2 And he laid hold on the dragon, that old serpent, which is the Devil, and Satan, and bound him a thousand years, 3 And cast him into the bottomless pit, and shut him up, and set a seal upon him, that he should deceive the nations no more, till the thousand years should be fulfilled: and after that he must be loosed a little season. 4 And I saw thrones, and they sat upon them, and judgment was given unto them: and I saw the souls of them that were beheaded for the witness of Jesus, and for the word of God, and which had not worshipped the beast, neither his image, neither had received his mark upon their foreheads, or in their hands; and they lived and reigned with Christ a thousand years. 5 But the rest of the dead lived not again until the thousand years were finished. This is the first resurrection.6 Blessed and holy is he that hath part in the first resurrection: on such the second death hath no power, but they shall be priests of God and of Christ, and shall reign with him a thousand years.

This millennial reign will bring the salvation of Israel,

**Ezekiel 37:21-22 (KJV)**

21 And say unto them, Thus saith the Lord God; Behold, I will take the children of Israel from among the heathen, whither they be gone, and will gather them on every side, and bring them into their own land: 22 And I will make them one nation in the land upon the mountains of Israel; and one king shall be king to them all: and they shall be no more two nations, neither shall they be divided into two kingdoms any more at all.

**Zephaniah 3:19-20 (KJV)**

19 Behold, at that time I will undo all that afflict thee: and I will save her that halteth, and gather her that was driven out; and I will get them praise and fame in every land where they have been

put to shame. 20 At that time will I bring you again, even in the time that I gather you: for I will make you a name and a praise among all people of the earth, when I turn back your captivity before your eyes, saith the Lord.

**Romans 11:26-27 (KJV)**
26 And so all Israel shall be saved: as it is written, There shall come out of Sion the Deliverer, and shall turn away ungodliness from Jacob: 27 For this is my covenant unto them, when I shall take away their sins.

and the establishment of universal peace.

**Isaiah 11:6-9 (KJV)**
6 The wolf also shall dwell with the lamb, and the leopard shall lie down with the kid; and the calf and the young lion and the fatling together; and a little child shall lead them. 7 And the cow and the bear shall feed; their young ones shall lie down together: and the lion shall eat straw like the ox. 8 And the sucking child shall play on the hole of the asp, and the weaned child shall put his hand on the cockatrice' den. 9 They shall not hurt nor destroy in all my holy mountain: for the earth shall be full of the knowledge of the Lord, as the waters cover the sea.

**Psalm 72:3-8 (KJV)**
3 The mountains shall bring peace to the people, and the little hills, by righteousness. 4 He shall judge the poor of the people, he shall save the children of the needy, and shall break in pieces the oppressor. 5 They shall fear thee as long as the sun and moon endure, throughout all generations. 6 He shall come down like rain upon the mown grass: as showers that water the earth. 7 In his days shall the righteous flourish; and abundance of peace so long as the moon endureth. 8 He shall have dominion also from sea to sea, and from the river unto the ends of the earth.

**Micah 4:3-4 (KJV)**
3 And he shall judge among many people, and rebuke strong nations afar off; and they shall beat their swords into plowshares, and their spears into pruning hooks: nation shall not lift up a sword against nation, neither shall they learn war any more. 4 But they shall sit every man under his vine and under his fig tree; and none shall make them afraid: for the mouth of the Lord of hosts hath spoken it.

*In this world in which we live today, where there is war on every continent, and famines, pestilences, earthquakes, and other disasters happening every day, it is hard to imagine the peace to come, captured in these verses.*

*Strife and conflict will end, and we, His church, will rule and reign with Him during this wonderful time of restoration.*

*During this time, we will have only a glimpse of how wonderful eternity will be, with our Lord and Savior.*

# CHAPTER 47
## SATAN'S LAST STAND

Remember, at the beginning of the Millennial Reign Satan was given a prison sentence of 1,000 years, and cast into the bottomless pit. (Revelation 20:1-3)

1. During this brief period between the Millennial Reign and the Great White Throne Judgment, the chains will be removed, and Satan will come up out of the bottomless pit, and he will once again set out to deceive people. (Revelation 20:7-10)

Revelation 20:3 tells us he will be released for "a little season" (KJV). It will be long enough for him to travel to the four quarters of the earth to gather together an army, to battle against Christ.

2. The reason? Well, remember those "Millennial Kingdom Children", those who did not take the Mark of the Beast during the Great Tribulation, are still clothed in their physical bodies. They have not yet put on their glorified bodies, and, as such, they still have a sinful nature.

Probably a billion or more children have been born to these "Millennial Kingdom Children" during the 1,000 year Millennial Reign. (Keep that in mind.)

One thousand years of peace, and, living under the reign of King Jesus has not erased their sinful nature.

Sacrifices have been made in the temple, and these "Millennial Kingdom Children" have been taught about the salvation of Jesus Christ, but Satan has not been able to offer them an alternative. They have seen the consequences of not serving God, as a result of the death penalty, but they have not actually been given the choice. Satan now being loosed, will afford them the opportunity to make a choice.

*Possibly, the only reason many (most) of these "Millennial Kingdom Children" have followed Christ is because of the fear of punishment (the public display of burning bodies). Now, through Satan's deceitful lies they will be given a choice, which will (for some) negate their fear (just like today).*

3. Satan's influence undoubtedly will spread like wildfire, and many will choose to follow him (Revelation 20:8). (As many as "the sand of the sea")

Think about that. Men and women, boys and girls, who have lived hundreds of years in a "Garden of Eden" type of environment, under the perfect rule of Jesus Christ, will choose to turn against God!

Then, Satan will form an army together, of those that choose him over Jesus, and he will try to overthrow the rule of Jesus Christ.

4. The results? Simple. Total victory for Jesus, and the Saints. That is one thing that never changes.

Revelation 20:9 tells us, "Fire came down out of heaven and devoured them." All that followed Satan will perish, during this final war.

Revelation 20:10 tells us, "The devil that deceived them was cast into the lake of fire and brimstone.", to be tormented day and night forever and forever. (Every second of every day, without time off, or vacation… forever!)

Again, how long will all of this take? The Bible says, "Satan will be loosed for a little season". Normally, when the Bible refers to a "season", it refers to a period of about three months.

*This week, if you love your unsaved friends, relatives, business associates, and neighbors, would you take a moment to share the good news of God's plan of salvation with them? Would you do your best to save them from a devil's hell? We must take this seriously! Satan is playing, and will continue to play, "for all the marbles".*

# CHAPTER 48
## THE GREAT WHITE THRONE JUDGMENT

This will be the only judgment, where every person, who has ever been born on planet earth, will be present. Not all to be judged, but will be present.

Let's first look at Revelation 20:11-15, "11 And I saw a great white throne and the one sitting on it. The earth and sky fled from his presence, but they found no place to hide. 12 I saw the dead, both great and small, standing before God's throne. And the books were opened, including the Book of Life. And the dead were judged according to what they had done, as recorded in the books. 13 The sea gave up its dead, and death and the grave gave up their dead. And all were judged according to their deeds. 14 Then death and the grave were thrown into the lake of fire. This lake of fire is the second death. 15 And anyone whose name was not found recorded in the Book of Life was thrown into the lake of fire."

And, then, Daniel 7:9-10, "9 I beheld till the thrones were cast down, and the Ancient of days did sit, whose garment was white as snow, and the hair of his head like the pure wool: his throne was like the fiery flame, and his wheels as burning fire. 10 A fiery stream issued and came forth from before him: thousand thousands ministered unto him, and ten thousand times ten thousand stood before him: the judgment was set, and the books were opened."

1. The Judge of this Throne will be Jesus. Some would question this because Revelation 20:12 says, "And I saw the dead, small and great, stand before God, and the books were opened."

Some would interpret "God" as God, the Father. Nevertheless, it is God the Son, according to John 5:22 and John 5:27; also Acts

10:40-42 and 2 Timothy 4:1. Jesus Christ will be the judge.

2. The Journey to the Throne will be by every man and women, boy and girl, ever conceived on earth. We, Christians, will only be there as spectators. We have already been "judged" at the Judgment Seat of Christ, so we will not be there to be judged.

3. The Jury of the Throne (Revelation 20:12) will be the "books" (plural) that "were opened", and "another book (singular) was opened… which is the Book of Life"

Some believe these "books" to be each individual's record book. I do not subscribe to this thought, because there is no scripture to support it. However, I do believe there are five books that God is using to record the actions of our lives. To wit:

a. The Book of Conscience. (Romans 2:14-16)
b. The Book of Words. (Matthew 12:36-37)
c. The Book of Secret Words & Works. (Romans 2:16 Ecclesiastes 12:14, 2 Chronicles 16:9, Zechariah 4:10 , Proverbs 15:3, and Hebrews 4:13)
d. The Book of Public Works. (Romans 2:5-6)
e. The Book of Life. (Philippians 4:3, Revelation 20:12 & 15, and 21:27)

4. The Judged of the Throne will be primarily for those who did not accept Jesus Christ as their Lord and Savior; however, look at what Revelation 20:15 says, "15 And whosoever was not found written in the book of life was cast into the lake of fire."

To me, this statement infers some names will be found, and others not found.

Hebrews 9:27 says, "It is appointed unto men once to die, but after this the judgment."

Those who accepted Jesus Christ during the Great Tribulation and during the Millennial Reign will also need to be "judged", and this is the only place I can see in Scripture where that could happen; so, I believe the above five books will be opened to them also, at the Great White Throne Judgment.

5. The Judgment of the Throne will be either "guilty" or "not guilty" (Revelation 20:15); and this judgment will be for life! (This is the second death.) (Revelation 20:14)

6. The Just of the Throne, will be those who accepted Jesus, and did not take the Mark of the Beast.

Consider Ezekiel 3:18-19.

Let's consider this event in another way in Chapter 49 next week.

# CHAPTER 49 THE FINAL JUDGMENT

There will be a final judgment in which the wicked dead will be raised and judged according to their works. Whosoever is not found written in the Book of Life, together with the devil and his angels, the beast and the false prophet, will be consigned to the everlasting punishment in the lake which burneth with fire and brimstone, which is the second death.

**Matthew 25:46 (KJV)**
46 And these shall go away into everlasting punishment: but the righteous into life eternal.

**Mark 9:43-48 (KJV)**
43 And if thy hand offend thee, cut it off: it is better for thee
to enter into life maimed, than having two hands to go into hell, into
the fire that never shall be quenched: 44 Where their worm dieth
not, and the fire is not quenched. 45 And if thy foot offend thee, cut
it off: it is better for thee to enter halt into life, than having two feet
to be cast into hell, into the fire that never shall be quenched: 46
Where their worm dieth not, and the fire is not quenched. 47 And
if thine eye offend thee, pluck it out: it is better for thee to enter
into the kingdom of God with one eye, than having two eyes to be
cast into hell fire: 48 Where their worm dieth not, and the fire is not
quenched.

**Revelation 19:20 (KJV)**
20 And the beast was taken, and with him the false prophet that wrought miracles before him, with which he deceived them that

had received the mark of the beast, and them that worshipped his image. These both were cast alive into a lake of fire burning with brimstone.

**Revelation 20:11-15 (KJV)**

11 And I saw a great white throne, and him that sat on it, from whose face the earth and the heaven fled away; and there was found no place for them. 12 And I saw the dead, small and great, stand before God; and the books were opened: and another book was opened, which is the book of life: and the dead were judged out of those things which were written in the books, according to their works. 13 And the sea gave up the dead which were in it; and death and hell delivered up the dead which were in them: and they were judged every man according to their works. 14 And death and hell were cast into the lake of fire. This is the second death. 15 And whosoever was not found written in the book of life was cast into the lake of fire.

**Revelation 21:8 (KJV)**

8 But the fearful, and unbelieving, and the abominable, and murderers, and whoremongers, and sorcerers, and idolaters, and all liars, shall have their part in the lake which burneth with fire and brimstone: which is the second death.

*It is my understanding and belief, that the church, you and I who have already stood before our Lord at the Judgment Seat of Christ, will sit in the gallery and watch as many of our friends, relatives, business associates, acquaintances, and neighbors are judged at the Great White Throne Judgment, are found guilty of not accepting Jesus as their Lord and Savior, and are cast into the Lake of Fire.*

*I have visions of these people looking around the gallery and their eye catching ours, as they cry out to us and ask, "Why didn't your warn me of this? Why did you not tell me?"*

***We <u>must</u> return to evangelism and discipleship.***

# CHAPTER 50
# THE NEW HEAVEN AND NEW EARTH
# (PART ONE)

"We, according to His promise, look for new heavens and a new earth wherein dwelleth righteousness."

**2 Peter 3:13 (KJV)**

13 Nevertheless we, according to his promise, look for new heavens and a new earth, wherein dwelleth righteousness.

**Revelation 21 (KJV)**

1 And I saw a new heaven and a new earth: for the first heaven
and the first earth were passed away; and there was no more sea.
2 And I John saw the holy city, new Jerusalem, coming down from
God out of heaven, prepared as a bride adorned for her husband.
3 And I heard a great voice out of heaven saying, Behold, the
tabernacle of God is with men, and he will dwell with them, and
they shall be his people, and God himself shall be with them, and
be their God. 4 And God shall wipe away all tears from their eyes;
and there shall be no more death, neither sorrow, nor crying, neither
shall there be any more pain: for the former things are passed
away. 5 And he that sat upon the throne said, Behold, I make all
things new. And he said unto me, Write: for these words are true
and faithful. 6 And he said unto me, It is done. I am Alpha and
Omega, the beginning and the end. I will give unto him that is athirst
of the fountain of the water of life freely. 7 He that overcometh
shall inherit all things; and I will be his God, and he shall be my
son. 8 But the fearful, and unbelieving, and the abominable, and

murderers, and whoremongers, and sorcerers, and idolaters, and all liars, shall have their part in the lake which burneth with fire and brimstone: which is the second death. 9 And there came unto me one of the seven angels which had the seven vials full of the seven last plagues, and talked with me, saying, Come hither, I will shew thee the bride, the Lamb's wife. 10 And he carried me away in the spirit to a great and high mountain, and shewed me that great city, the holy Jerusalem, descending out of heaven from God, 11 Having the glory of God: and her light was like unto a stone most precious, even like a jasper stone, clear as crystal; 12 And had a wall great and high, and had twelve gates, and at the gates twelve angels, and names written thereon, which are the names of the twelve tribes of the children of Israel: 13 On the east three gates; on the north three gates; on the south three gates; and on the west three gates. 14 And the wall of the city had twelve foundations, and in them the names of the twelve apostles of the Lamb. 15 And he that talked with me had a golden reed to measure the city, and the gates thereof, and the wall thereof.16 And the city lieth foursquare, and the length is as large as the breadth: and he measured the city with the reed, twelve thousand furlongs. The length and the breadth and the height of it are equal. 17 And he measured the wall thereof, an hundred and forty and four cubits, according to the measure of a man, that is, of the angel. 18 And the building of the wall of it was of jasper: and the city was pure gold, like unto clear glass. 19 And the foundations of the wall of the city were garnished with all manner of precious stones. The first foundation was jasper; the second, sapphire; the third, a chalcedony; the fourth, an emerald; 20 The fifth, sardonyx; the sixth, sardius; the seventh, chrysolyte; the eighth, beryl; the ninth, a topaz; the tenth, a chrysoprasus; the eleventh, a jacinth; the twelfth, an amethyst. 21 And the twelve gates were twelve pearls: every several gate was of one pearl: and the street of the city was pure gold, as it were transparent glass. 22 And I saw no temple therein: for the Lord God Almighty and the Lamb are the temple of it. 23 And the city had no need of the sun, neither of the moon, to shine in it: for the glory of God did lighten it, and the Lamb is the light thereof. 24 And the nations of them which are saved shall walk in the light of it: and the kings of the earth do bring their glory and honour into it. 25 And the gates of it shall not be shut at all by day: for there shall be no night there. 26 And they shall bring the glory and honour of the nations into it. 27 And there shall in no wise enter into it any thing that defileth, neither whatsoever worketh abomination, or maketh a lie: but they which are written in the Lamb's book of life.

**Revelation 22 (KJV)**

1 And he shewed me a pure river of water of life, clear as crystal,
proceeding out of the throne of God and of the Lamb. 2 In the midst of
the street of it, and on either side of the river, was there the tree of life,
which bare twelve manner of fruits, and yielded her fruit every month:
and the leaves of the tree were for the healing of the nations. 3 And
there shall be no more curse: but the throne of God and of the Lamb
shall be in it; and his servants shall serve him: 4 And they shall see his
face; and his name shall be in their foreheads. 5 And there shall be no
night there; and they need no candle, neither light of the sun; for the
Lord God giveth them light: and they shall reign for ever and ever. 6
And he said unto me, These sayings are faithful and true: and the Lord
God of the holy prophets sent his angel to shew unto his servants the
things which must shortly be done. 7 Behold, I come quickly: blessed
is he that keepeth the sayings of the prophecy of this book. 8 And I
John saw these things, and heard them. And when I had heard and seen,
I fell down to worship before the feet of the angel which shewed me
these things. 9 Then saith he unto me, See thou do it not: for I am thy
fellowservant, and of thy brethren the prophets, and of them which keep
the sayings of this book: worship God. 10 And he saith unto me, Seal
not the sayings of the prophecy of this book: for the time is at hand. 11
He that is unjust, let him be unjust still: and he which is filthy, let him
be filthy still: and he that is righteous, let him be righteous still: and he
that is holy, let him be holy still. 12 And, behold, I come quickly; and
my reward is with me, to give every man according as his work shall
be. 13 I am Alpha and Omega, the beginning and the end, the first and
the last. 14 Blessed are they that do his commandments, that they may
have right to the tree of life, and may enter in through the gates into
the city. 15 For without are dogs, and sorcerers, and whoremongers,
and murderers, and idolaters, and whosoever loveth and maketh a lie.
16 I Jesus have sent mine angel to testify unto you these things in the
churches. I am the root and the offspring of David, and the bright and
morning star. 17 And the Spirit and the bride say, Come. And let him
that heareth say, Come. And let him that is athirst come. And whosoever
will, let him take the water of life freely. 18 For I testify unto every
man that heareth the words of the prophecy of this book, If any man
shall add unto these things, God shall add unto him the plagues that
are written in this book: 19 And if any man shall take away from the
words of the book of this prophecy, God shall take away his part out of
the book of life, and out of the holy city, and from the things which are
written in this book. 20 He which testifieth these things saith, Surely I
come quickly. Amen. Even so, come, Lord Jesus. 21 The grace of our
Lord Jesus Christ be with you all. Amen.

# Chapter 51
# The New Heaven and New Earth
# (Part two)

I want you to think about this with me, and I do not present this as a firm conclusion, but merely to provoke thought.

The Bible says this earth is going to melt away with a fervent heat, and we are to look for a new heaven and a new earth.

Now, think of this: we are referred to as a "new creature" when we are saved. 2 Co. 5:17 says, "Old things are passed away, behold all things are become new." Yet, we are the same physical person, in the same flesh (body), but we have a new heart (spirit) within us, and a new direction, and new purpose.

Let me ask you, can this earth experience a "washing by fire", and become a new earth?

Speaking of the flood, 2 Peter 3:6 says, "Whereby the world that then was, being overflowed with water, perished:". Perish means to die, to succumb, to decease, to expire, to pass away; to depart this life… you get the picture.

In Noah's day, the world that was then, was flooded, and the Bible says, "perished". Nevertheless, it wasn't completely eliminated, it was just revitalized, and it became the new earth, after it was washed by water; just as you and I became new creatures after we were washed by the blood of Jesus Christ.

Will you agree that the "new earth" can, in fact, appear on this same planet?

One more scripture for your consideration: Ecclesiastes 1:4, "One generation passeth away, and another generation cometh: but the earth abideth for ever."

"…but the earth abideth forever." Think about that.

Think about it this way: when you pass away, do you cease to exist?

Absolutely not! If you are a Christian, your spirit will continue to live on (God-consciousness). If you are not a Christian, your soul will continue to live on (self-consciousness).

So… in the Bible, the term "pass away" does not necessarily mean to "cease to exist".

John wrote, (Rev. 21:1) " And I saw a new heaven and a new earth: for the first heaven and the first earth were passed away; and there was no more sea."

"…were passed away…", but did not cease to exist.

One more thought. The new heaven and the new earth do not come down from heaven, only the new Jerusalem does.

Now, let's consider the new earth:

a. It will have no sea (Rev. 21:1), which will create a great deal more surface area.

b. There will be no more hell. (Rev. 20:14)

c. There will be no trace of sin (no reminder of sin). (Isaiah 65:17)

Also, notice Revelation 21:1 says (in part) "… new heaven… for the first heaven…". Heaven, singular (not plural). Today, the first heaven is our atmosphere (Genesis 1:8 – shaw-mah-yim), the second heaven is the space above our atmosphere, where the planets are located (Genesis 22:17 – shaw-mah-yin), and the third heaven is beyond our vision, where God dwells (2 Co. 12:2 – oo-ran-os, meaning "elevated" and implying "eternity".)

When John saw a new heaven, he was referring to a new atmosphere around the fire-washed-earth.

It is my thought, that while every person ever created is assembled in the 3rd heaven, for the Great White Throne Judgment, that God will purify and purge this earth, and the 1st heaven. Then, as soon as the last sinner is sentenced to the Lake of Fire, we are going for another outer-space ride, as we descend (again) from the 3rd heaven, possibly "on" the New Jerusalem; and, in that moment He will fulfill Revelation 21:4, " And God shall wipe away all tears from their eyes; and there shall be no more death, neither sorrow, nor crying, neither shall there be any more pain: for the former things are passed away."

Just for fun, consider with me the tremendous size of the New Jerusalem. Revelation 21:16 says, "And the city lieth foursquare, and the length is as large as the breadth: and he measured the city with the reed, twelve thousand furlongs. The length and the breadth and the height of it are equal."

A furlong is 220 yards. Multiplied by 3, to equate into feet, would equal 660 feet. 660 feet times 12,000 (furlongs) would equal 7,920,000 feet, divided by 5280 feet (one mile) would equal 1,500 miles (exactly).

That would be approximately the distance from Boston to Miami (north to south) and, Philadelphia to Denver (east to west). The length and the breadth and the height of the New Jerusalem are equal, so, therefore, that 1,500 miles is CUBED. Wow! (1 Corinthians 2:9 comes to my mind about now.)

Consider further the New Jerusalem:

a. It will have unique foundations. (Rev. 21:19-20) A beautiful rainbow of colors.

b. It will have walls of Jasper. (Rev. 21:17-18)

c. It will have a single pearl for each of the twelve gates. (Rev. 21:12-13 & 21a)

d. The city will have a golden street. (Rev. 21:21b) One single street. Transparent from level to level.

e. The city will have a bright light. (Rev. 21:23) Jesus Christ will illuminate the city.

f. It will have a pure river, and, a tree of life. (Rev. 22:1-2)

g. The city will not have a temple. (Rev. 21:22) "…for the Lord God Almighty and the Lamb are the temple."

And, the final recorded words of Jesus are captured in Revelation 22:20, "Surely I come quickly. Amen.")

In closing, let me repeat John's last words in this prophecy, "The grace of our Lord Jesus Christ be with you all. Amen."

# CHAPTER 52
# PERPETUATING DISCIPLESHIP

## THE GREAT COMMISSION

**MATTHEW 28:16-20 (NIV)**
16 Then the eleven disciples went to Galilee, to the mountain
where Jesus had told them to go. 17 When they saw him, they
worshiped him; but some doubted. 18 Then Jesus came to them and
said, "All authority in heaven and on earth has been given to me.
19Therefore go and make disciples of all nations, baptizing them
in the name of the Father and of the Son and of the Holy Spirit, 20
and teaching them to obey everything I have commanded you. And
surely I am with you always, to the very end of the age."

On this final week of what is intended to be a 52-week long study, I would ask you, the discipler, and the disciple, to discuss ways you will both perpetuate the disciple-making process, as each of you continue to grow in the grace and in the knowledge of our Lord and Savior, Jesus Christ.

Talk about it together. Pray about it together. And, then, "Go Make (Pentecostal) Disciples"!

GO MAKE (PENTECOSTAL) DISCIPLES

PUBLISHED by PARABLES
Earthly Stories with a Heavenly Meaning